Grammar
Smart
Junior

Grammar Smart

Junior

Good Grammar Made Easy

by Liz Buffa

Random House, Inc. New York
www.randomhouse.com

ISBN: 0-375-76259-0
Second Edition
Manufactured in the United States of America.
10 9 8 7 6 5 4 3

ACKNOWLEDGMENTS

The author would like to thank the following for their invaluable contributions: Michael Freedman, Marcia Lerner, Diane Fagiola, and Marissa La Magna for their emotional support.

And thanks of course to Dominick, David, and Paul, for their patience and proofreading.

CONTENTS

Introduction ix

Chapter 1 The Names of Things......................1
   Nouns 3
   Pronouns 6
   Verbs..8
   Adjectives 10
   Adverbs..12
   Prepositions 15
   Conjunctions...17
   Interjections 19

Chapter 2 The Sentence 27
   The Subject 28
   The Predicate 32
   Phrases 35
   Clauses 38
   Simple, Compound, and Complex Sentences......40

Chapter 3 More About Nouns 47
   Types of Nouns......................................48
   Pronouns 58

Chapter 4 More About Verbs.........................75
   Types of Verbs.......................................75

Chapter 5 More About Adjectives, Adverbs, Prepositions, and Other Details 95

Adjectives and Adverbs 95
Modifiers and Prepositions.............................100
Other Details About Grammar 109

Chapter 6 Punctuation...................................115

The Period 116
The Comma 117
The Question Mark 120
The Exclamation Point 121
The Semicolon 122
The Colon 123
Quotation Marks..123
The Dash 125
Parentheses 125

Chapter 7 The Princeton Review List of Commonly Misused and Confused Words 129

Learning to Spell Correctly 129
Diction 132

Cool Books for Cool Readers 145

Glossary 149

Answers 157

About the Author 191

Introduction

WHY SHOULD I LEARN ABOUT GRAMMAR?

Some of you are better at fashion, some of you are better at reading, and some of you are better at making great lay-ups on the basketball court. Whatever your skills are and whatever it is you like, you most certainly have to talk to people and write from time to time. Communication is important, and using proper grammar is also important for two reasons: *to be clear* and *to sound educated*. Huh?

Let us explain. Many of the grammar rules you will encounter are there to make your life *easier*. You need to communicate with people, right? Well, let's say you write this in a paper:

> I told Maria that I like U2's new CD more than her.

Now, did you just insult your friend by saying that you like a CD more than you like her? Or did you just say that you like this particular CD more than she likes it? Well, to be honest, according to the rules of grammar, you told her that you like this CD more than you like her, and that's probably not what you meant.

That's the first thing grammar helps you do—if you use your words carefully and correctly, you will avoid misunderstandings.

NOW, ABOUT THE SOUNDING EDUCATED PART . . .

Sure, we want you to speak and write perfectly all the time because there is beauty in doing so. But if beauty alone is not enough incentive for you, how about things like getting good grades and good jobs? You know the unfortunate truth: No matter how wonderful your thoughts are, if they're written with lots of grammatical errors, you won't get a good grade. And no matter how wonderful a person you are, if you go into a job interview years from now and say

> "I just know I done good on that
> test you gave me, sir!"

well, you won't be getting that job. So knowing proper grammar is important for many reasons.

WELL, WHAT'S THIS BOOK ABOUT?

We want to teach you good grammar and make it incredibly *clear, easy* and, most of all, *interesting*. We don't necessarily expect you to read this book from cover to cover; some of you will just use it for reference when you have a specific question. That's fine. We'll remind you from time to time about which rules are *really* important rules that you should always follow no matter what, and which rules are the ones that only English teachers will give you a hard time about.

BUT I HATE GRAMMAR . . .

Okay, it's not your fault. Grammar can be boring, and it doesn't make much sense when you are asked to speak one way, but often hear English spoken in a completely different way. That's confusing. When you watch TV, read magazines, look at advertisements, and listen to music, you are constantly exposed to bad grammar.

Now don't get us wrong. We have nothing against bad grammar in things like music or advertising. Sometimes using the wrong word sounds better when you're writing lyrics to a song or jingle. But you aren't a famous rock star (yet). We're going to help you learn the difference between good and bad grammar and help you write better school reports and get higher scores on tests. You should know that bad grammar is definitely not okay in school.

TESTS?

Sure, tests. Even if you haven't had them yet, pretty soon you'll be called upon to answer questions about grammar: Your teacher will ask you what a dependent clause is, or to identify the errors in a poorly written sentence. Both of these things will be simple if you start now by getting an ear for good grammar. What does that mean? If you have an ear for music, you might recognize immediately if a song is by Madonna or Janet Jackson. If you have an ear for good grammar, you will recognize when something just doesn't sound right.

BUT WAIT A MINUTE . . . MY COMPUTER HAS A GRAMMAR CHECKER AND A SPELL CHECKER!

Okay, you caught us. There is, in fact, a grammar checker and a spell checker on many word processing programs. And some silly people now believe that there will be no reason for kids to learn grammar and spelling in the future, because it will simply be a matter of hitting a key and letting the computer change your wonderful, yet grammatically incorrect thoughts into perfect, sparkling English. Well, we hate to break this to you, but *grammar and spelling programs don't always work.*

Really. Would we lie to you? Okay, spell checkers work pretty well. They'll pick up some misspellings.

But first you have to spell a word *sort of* right for a spell checker to correct it. If you're *way* off, it won't know what word you're talking about. (It is only a machine, after all.) And it won't pick up misspellings in which you turn one word into another (for example, if you spell *you're* as *your*). Both are correctly spelled words, and the spell checker only picks out words that don't appear in its dictionary.

And those grammar checks? Forget them. As of now, they are pretty much useless. If you tried to use a grammar check on a report or essay, chances are you'd be more lost after you were done than before you started.

Sorry to break the news to you. Just be grateful we're here to help.

How to Use this Book

This book is arranged so that it will be easy to follow and fun to read. You can read it through a little at a time and test yourself with the quizzes that follow each topic. They are there for you to figure out if you get the idea. You don't have to get every question right to feel good about yourself. If you get most of the questions right on the quizzes, you're doing well. While you're doing that, you can follow the story of a group of friends who were just hanging out one day when they found their ticket to adventureland.

Those of you who open the book only to find an answer to a specific question should appreciate that we go in order, from basic definitions to more detailed points of grammar to common errors and tips. You may find yourself reading a little bit ahead just to see how things really work in this complicated machine we call grammar. It's not so bad after all—and when you're done, you'll be rewarded with the ability to speak and write very well.

Chapter 1
The Names of Things

To learn about grammar you have to learn the names of things. The parts of speech are the pieces you use to put sentences and paragraphs together. To put them together properly, you need to know what each piece is called and what role it plays.

So what's the point? Well, we won't fool you. Chances are good that, unless you become a contestant on *Jeopardy* in your adult life, you won't be called upon regularly to name the parts of speech. So do we really care if you can name the parts of speech with your eyes closed? No, not really. We are defining these terms so that you will understand what we are talking about throughout the book. And chances are that, as a student, you will need to know these terms when your teacher gives you one of those nasty little quizzes that teachers so love to give.

If you play baseball, you don't really need to know the name of a squeeze play to be able to make one, right? And you don't need to know the name of a reflexive pronoun to use one properly. But if you look up at your coach blankly when he asks you to make a squeeze play, he may think, "Hey, I'm not sure if this kid really knows how to play baseball."

Okay, so words are put into eight different categories depending on the roles they play in sentences. The eight parts of speech are

nouns

pronouns

verbs

adjectives

adverbs

prepositions

conjunctions

interjections

If you are confused, the easiest way to find out the part of speech of a word is to look up the word in a dictionary. A dictionary definition will include information about what part of speech a word is. For example:

fly, n.; pl. flies. 1. a housefly; any of a group of
　　insects with two transparent wings,
　　including the housefly and the Mayfly. 2. a
　　device made of feathers, silk, etc., to
　　resemble an insect, used in fishing as a bait.

Now, as you can see, this is the definition of *fly* that means an insect or fishing lure. That little *n.* after the word tells you that fly is a noun, and the *pl.* tells you that the plural of fly is flies. It gives you two definitions. (The first is always the most common use of the word.)

But there's another definition of fly that means something completely different.

fly, v.; flew, pt.; flown, pp. 1. to move through the air, with wings, as a bird flies, or by airplane. 2. to operate an airplane. 3. to float in the air, as a kite or flag does.

This definition of *fly* indicates that fly can also be a verb. It also gives you some of the different tenses of the verb. We'll get into those later in Chapter 4. For now you should know that a word might only, and always, be one part of speech, or it may be more than one part of speech depending on the way it is used in a sentence.

NOUNS

A noun is a person, place, thing, or idea.

Person: Pierre, Juanita, firefighter, friend, Mom

Place: school, home, Greasy Spoon Diner

Thing: cat, calendar, stereo, CD

Idea: truth, justice, the American way

There are two general categories of nouns: common nouns and proper nouns.

A common noun is a word that names any person, place, or thing. A proper noun names a specific person, place, or thing. Compare the two.

Common noun	Proper noun
girl	Maria
teacher	Mr. Escobar
city	Chicago
state	Alaska
college	Michigan State

What do you notice about common nouns and proper nouns? Proper nouns are always capitalized and common nouns are not (unless they begin a sentence, of course).

In the following paragraph, the nouns are in italics.

> *Jem* stayed moody and silent for a *week*. As *Atticus* had once advised me to do, I tried to climb into *Jem's skin* and walk around in it: if I had not gone to the *Radley Place* at two in the *morning*, my *funeral* would have been held the next *afternoon*. So I left *Jem* alone and tried not to bother him.
>
> from *To Kill A Mockingbird*, Harper Lee

✍ QUIZ #1 ✍
What's this Ticket?

Underline the common nouns and circle the proper nouns in the following passage.

It was a hot day around the old clubhouse. Sondra, Barnaby, Babette, Taylor, Bridget, and Jennifer had been hanging around watching television most of that week—it seemed too hot to do anything else.

"Man, what I wouldn't do to spend a week on Gilligan's Island," said Barnaby. "First of all, I wouldn't mind meeting the Professor, and secondly, it would be nice and cool there."

"Forget *Gilligan's Island*," answered Jennifer. "Give me *Friends* any day. I'd love to hang with Rachel, meet Joey, bum around with that whole gang. Their lives seem like so much fun."

"You guys are weird," said Taylor, dreamily. "Give me a nice, happy family like the one on the *Brady Bunch*. Now there are some fun people I'd like to spend a week with."

"What's this silver ticket on the floor?" asked Bridget. "I've never seen anything like it before."

PRONOUNS

Okay, now that you know what a noun is, you'll be able to recognize pronouns. Pronouns are used as stand-ins for nouns—sort of like stuntpeople for actors in a movie. Think of how horrible and awkward your sentences would sound without pronouns to stand in for nouns every now and then. For example, instead of saying

> Marcia told John that Marcia liked
> John's story better than Marcia
> liked Marcia's story.

you get to say

> Marcia told John that she liked his
> story better than she liked hers.

Obviously, pronouns make your sentences a little smoother. Using them means you don't have to repeat the nouns over and over again, when we all know what noun you're referring to. The italicized words in the following paragraph are pronouns.

We lived on the main residential street in town—
Atticus, Jem and *I*, plus Calpurnia, our cook. Jem
and *I* found our father satisfactory: *he* played with
us, read to *us*, and treated *us* with courteous
detachment.

from *To Kill a Mockingbird*, Harper Lee

✍ QUIZ #2 ✍
A Ticket to Adventure

**Underline the pronouns in the following
passage.**

"It says, 'This is your ticket to adventure. If
you hold onto it tightly, you will be
transported to the television show of your
dreams. To escape from your adventure, say
the words *anna banana*,'" said Jennifer.

"That's strange. What do you suppose it
means?" wondered Babette.

"I suppose that it means exactly what it says.
Where would we like to go?" answered
Barnaby, being logical as usual.

"I would like to go to Central Perk to hang
out with the cast of *Friends*," Jennifer said.
"They would all love me!"

"I don't know about that," said Taylor.

But it was too late. The clubhouse began to
rattle. They all held onto the nearest pieces, of
furniture. Before they could say "Ross and
Rachel," they were off.

VERBS

A verb is a word that expresses an action or a state of being. A verb is one of the most important words in a sentence—you cannot express a complete thought without one.

The action may be

Physical: I *ran* through the field.

Josh *played* football on Saturday morning.

Mental: I *thought* you'd be here.

Paul *felt* sick.

As a "state of being," a verb expresses what something is, or its condition, rather than a real action.

State of being: Jane *is* happy.

Jordan *was* successful.

In the following paragraph, all the verbs are in italics.

Lennie *went* behind the tree and *brought* out a litter of dried leaves and twigs. He *threw* them in a heap on the old ash pile and *went* back for more and more. It *was* almost night now. A dove's wings *whistled* over the water. George *walked* to the fire pile and *lighted* the dry leaves. The flame *crackled* up among the twigs and *fell* to work. George *undid* his bundle and *brought* out three cans of beans.

from *Of Mice and Men*, John Steinbeck

Friends, Here We Come!

Underline the verbs in the following passage.

Jennifer opened the door slowly. The coffee shop was filled with customers. Soon, the kids heard a familiar voice.

"What is this ugly house doing in Central Perk?" Monica asked harshly.

"Uh, we are not exactly sure ourselves," answered Jennifer. "Is this really Central Perk?"

"You bet, Sweetie," answered Rachel. "And if you don't get this broken-down old clubhouse out of our coffee shop, we will force you out."

"Rachel, what is the problem?" Joey entered the scene.

"No problem, Joey. There is just a bunch of rude, noisy kids trespassing in our cool hangout. I am sure they will find their way out of here before you can wink an eye." Rachel turned on her heel, stomped up to the counter, and ordered a latté.

"Hmm, what do you think of Rachel now?" asked Sondra.

"Ugh," answered Jennifer. "*Anna banana.*"

ADJECTIVES

It would be a dreary world indeed without adjectives. As a matter of fact, it would just be a world, because there'd be no words like *dreary*. Now, you may have thought that nouns and pronouns and verbs were just okay, but adjectives, well, that's another story. In grammar and writing, the fun really starts when you get to *describe* things, and that's where adjectives come in. An adjective is a word that describes or modifies a noun. An adjective answers questions about a noun. For example:

Noun: Book—What kind of book is it?

It is a *red* book.

It is a *large* book.

Noun: House—Whose house is it?

It is *my* house.

Daisy's house is down the street.

Noun: Computer—Which computer is it?

Which computer are you working on?

What computer did you sit at?

This computer is my favorite.

That computer is broken.

In the following paragraph, all the adjectives are in italics.

He stood frowning as the ring of *blue-white* fire flickered and danced; he even looked *cold*, with a *dark, pinched* look round the bones of his face. "They bring in the *deep* cold," he said, half to himself. "The cold of the void, of *black* space . . ."

from *The Dark is Rising*, Susan Cooper

✍ QUIZ #4 ✍
Just Sit Right Back and You'll Hear a Tale . . .

Underline the adjectives in the following passage.

The clubhouse may have been shabby, but it was sturdy enough to get them back home in a wink.

"Wow," said Jennifer, "this silver ticket really works! We should think hard about the next exciting place we'd like to go."

"We could go somewhere cool," offered Barnaby.

"Somewhere fun," said Babette.

"Somewhere exotic," said Taylor.

"Hmm, Central Perk wasn't exotic enough for you?" asked a nervous Bridget. She snapped her cherry gum and blew an enormous bubble.

"No, let's try someplace new and different," answered Babette.

"Someplace where there are cool ocean breezes, perhaps?" asked Barnaby.

"Yeah, cool, fresh breezes. That sounds pretty nice." Taylor looked off into the steamy street.

"Maybe *Gilligan's Island*?" Barnaby grabbed the silver ticket and rubbed it.

ADVERBS

Adverbs are like the workhorses of describing words. While an adjective describes a noun, an adverb is a word that describes or modifies a verb, an adjective, or even another adverb. Adverbs answer questions about verbs, adjectives, or other adverbs. What does that mean? Here are some examples.

David *always* eats a lot.

Diane did well *enough* on her exam.

The adverbs above answer the question "how?" The first adverb describes the verb *eats* and tells you *how often* David eats. The second adverb describes the adverb *well* and tells you *how well* Diane did.

He will be here *later*.

Mr. Bradley will arrive *soon*.

The adverbs above answer the question "when?" The first adverb describes the verb *will be* and tells you *when* he will be here. The second adverb describes the verb *will arrive* and tells you *when* Mr. Bradley will arrive.

Evan ran *behind*.

Mary Ann looked *there*.

These adverbs answer the question "where?" The first one describes the verb *ran* and tells you *where* Evan ran. The second one describes the verb *looked* and tells you *where* Mary Ann looked.

I *really, really* want to go to the movies.

Peter *actually* will go along with me.

These adverbs are used for emphasis. In the first sentence the adverbs emphasize the verb *want*. The adverb in the second sentence emphasizes the verb *will go*.

Dominick runs *swiftly*.

Dan sings *happily*.

Adverbs like the ones above are the most common. They end in *-ly* and answer the question "how?" How does Dominick run? *Swiftly*. How does Dan sing? *Happily*.

Many adverbs end in *-ly*, but, as you can see, many do not.

✍ QUIZ #5 ✍
The Professor and Barnaby

Underline the adverbs in the following passage.

"Gilligan!" yelled Mary Ann. She ran breathlessly up the beach and into the woods.

The kids were perched clumsily in the nearest coconut tree.

"What's the matter, Mary Ann? You seem very upset." Gilligan ran quickly toward her.

"No, it's just that I heard something—a very funny kind of crash. I'm a little scared, Gilligan. Let's go get the Professor."

"The Professor!" whispered Barnaby excitedly. "I have always wanted to meet him. He's one of the great minds in television history."

"Sure, if he's so very smart, how come he never got them off this stupid island?" Bridget snapped her gum furiously.

"Sssh, Bridget, here he comes!" Barnaby pointed at the figure moving slowly through the clump of trees.

"Professor, we're really stuck. Here! Up in this tree!" called Barnaby.

"My, my, how did you kids get stuck up in a coconut tree?" pondered the Professor. "And who are you, anyway? How can we be sure that you aren't a bunch of spies, sent here by some of our enemies?"

"Spies? Professor, I am your very biggest fan," cried Barnaby.

"Oh, really?" asked the Professor. "And how is it that you know my name?"

PREPOSITIONS

A preposition is a word that shows how a noun or pronoun is related to another word in a sentence. It gives the noun's relation in place, direction, or time. For example:

Place: Alice was *at* her desk.

She was *behind* her friend.

At and *behind* place Alice in relation to her desk and her friend.

Direction: Martha came *from* the pizza parlor.

I was going *to* the movies.

To and *from* give you the directions Martha and I are going in relation to something else (here, the pizza parlor and the movies).

Time: I'd rather go skiing *in* February.

Melanie will be home *at* 3:00 P.M.

In and *at* both connect the nouns to time—February and 3:00 P.M.

Here are some examples of prepositions.

Place: around, through, over, above, in, after, at, behind, under, on, by

Direction: from, to, away, after, into

Time: before, by, at, after, on, in

Some prepositions, such as *about* and *of*, show relationships that might not have anything to do with place, direction, or time.

Court Martial on Gilligan's Island

Circle the prepositions in the following passage.

Once in the hut, the kids began to panic. "How did we get ourselves into this?" asked Taylor.

"Don't worry—I'll get us out of this trouble," Barnaby said with confidence. "I can reason with the Professor."

"Okay, kids, we don't know who you are, but we suspect that you are a bunch of spies. How else would you all know our names?" said the Skipper, pacing around the room as he spoke.

"I can prove we're not spies!" cried Babette. "I don't know anything about this stupid show! I only watch *Beverly Hills 90210*."

"A likely story!" answered Ginger. "I've been to Beverly Hills, of course, and I'm sure it would be very boring to just sit and watch it all day long. Only a spy would do that! They're trying to learn all of our customs."

"Let's feed them to the crocodiles!" yelled Mary Ann.

"No, let's send them out on a raft!" countered the Professor.

"Forget it!" Barnaby rolled his eyes. "*Anna banana.*"

CONJUNCTIONS

A conjunction is a joining word. You might say

> Juanita went to school. She took a test.

You could make those two sentences into one with a conjunction.

> Juanita went to school *and* she took a test.

or even

> Juanita went to school *and* took a test.

Conjunctions are pretty easy to spot. They join two or more things together in a sentence. Some conjunctions work alone.

> If you go to the store, take the dog *and* the cat.

> I wanted to bring our goldfish, *but* my mother said no.

> If you buy the goldfish *or* the snails, I'll be happy.

> *Although* I like snails, I prefer goldfish.

(Notice with that last example that conjunctions don't always come between the things they join. *Although* joins the clauses *I like snails* and *I prefer goldfish.*)

Some conjunctions work in pairs.

> *Neither* Ollie *nor* Stan would have eaten that goldfish!

> *Either* goldfish *or* snails are delicious when cooked with garlic.

> *Not only* garlic, *but also* onions, are necessary when preparing such delicacies!

✍ QUIZ #7 ✍
Wilma!

Underline the conjunctions in the following passage.

"Ugh," Barnaby said, rolling his eyes as they landed back at home. "Neither *Friends* nor *Gilligan's Island* was at all what I'd imagined."

"Maybe we'd better forget all about this ticket and traveling for today," Bridget said as she snapped her gum.

"Not only are you guys boring, but you also lack imagination," Sondra said. "Let's go someplace, I don't know, unreal. How about Bedrock?"

"Where?" asked Taylor. He had never heard of *Gilligan's Island* or Bedrock. This day was beginning to tire him out.

"You know—Fred, Wilma, Betty, and Barney. Bedrock!"

"Barney? You mean that large, purple

dinosaur. I don't think so!" Babette wrinkled her nose and threw her hands up in disgust.

"I'm not talking about the purple dinosaur, Babette. I'm talking about Barney from the cartoon *The Flintstones*. C'mon, either you give me that ticket or I'll never speak to you again."

"Here—do what you want—I give up," Babette said, tossing the ticket at Sondra's feet.

"Wilma—I always wanted to meet you and Betty," Sondra said as she rubbed the ticket.

The walls of the clubhouse began to shimmer. The kids felt weird and wobbly. They were turning into cartoon characters!

INTERJECTIONS

Hey! Yo! Cool! It's interjection time. Interjections are easy and fun and have no real rules, which makes them especially great. An interjection is a word that usually stands alone that you can add for emphasis.

> *Wow!* What a great new haircut.

> *Yecch!* You look stupid.

> *Ha!* What do you know about it?

Not all interjections are followed by exclamation points. Sometimes, words that act like introductions are considered interjections. For example:

> *Really,* you should cut your hair.

> *Yes,* you are right.

✍ QUIZ #8 ✍

We Forgot About the Dinosaurs

Ha! Find the interjections! Underline them!

"Wow! Barney," called Fred, "check this out."

"What is it, Fred?" Barney leaned over the stone fence between their houses. "Yikes! What's that?"

"I'm not sure Barn—it looks like some kind of strange wooden house. Who ever heard of a wooden house?"

The kids nervously peered out the window.

"Cool! We're cartoons. Look, Sondra, there's Fred and Barney. They're pointing at us. Wave."

"Hey, you kids. What are you doing in our tree? Wilma! Call the Rock Police!"

"Oh!" Wilma said as she walked out into the yard. "What's going on here, Fred?"

Dino came bounding into the yard. "Yip, yip!" He jumped up at the base of the tree, clawing furiously at the bottom of the clubhouse.

"They don't seem very friendly, either," Sondra said as she shook her head.

"Oh, well, *anna banana*."

Party On with Parts of Speech

Okay, you've finished learning about the parts of speech. Now you can play the parts-of-speech games. You'll need a friend or two. Ask each person to call out a word that is the part of speech required in each blank. Don't tell your friends the title or the subject of the story. The more creative the words are, the funnier the final story will be. Read the story out loud once the blanks are all filled in.

✍ PARTS OF SPEECH GAME #1 ✍
Candy Warning

Warning: Candy Can Be Hazardous to Your Health

Washington, DC—The National Health Department released a (noun)_____ warning young (plural noun)_____ about the dangers of (verb ending in -*ing*) _____ candy.

"Many people don't realize that candy contains (noun)_____," warned a senior official at the department.

"If you eat (adjective) _____ candy three or more times a (noun) _____, you will jeopardize your chances of growing up (adjective) _____."

"(interjection)_____!" proclaimed a group of (nouns) _____. "We love to (verb) _____ candy. We (verb) _____ it almost once a day!"

To minimize the danger, officials advise that you (verb)_____ your candy (adverb)_____ and (verb)_____ immediately (preposition)_____ your house.

✍ PARTS OF SPEECH GAME #2 ✍
School Survival Guide

If you want to make it through a (noun) _____ at school, you should always remember to (verb) _____ your teachers. If you (verb)_____ your (adjective)_____ teachers, you can expect to (verb)_____ every single time.

How do you (verb)_____ time and time again? (interjection) _____! Call your teacher a (noun) _____ and (singular pronoun) _____ will really (verb) _____ your effort. Another surefire way to (verb) _____ your (adjective)_____ teacher is to (adverb) _____ (verb) _____ that teacher in front of the whole (group noun) _____.

✍ PARTS OF SPEECH GAME #3 ✍
A Trip to the Moon

Are you interested in (verb ending in *-ing*)
_____ to the moon? Well, you will
need a/an (adjective) _____ (noun)
_____ and your favorite (noun)
_____. Take these things and (verb)
_____ them together in your best
(noun) _____.

"(interjection) _____!" you may
say, "Is that all I need to (verb) _____
to the moon?"

"(interjection) _____ is what I say
to you. All it takes is a couple of (nouns)
_____ and a few very (adjective)
_____ (nouns) _____ and
soon you'll be (adverb) _____ on
your way! Bon voyage!

Review

There are *eight* parts of speech. Give a quick definition and an example of each one. The answers are on pages 165–166.

1. _____

_____

_____

_____

2. _____

_____

_____

_____

3. _____

_____

_____

_____

4. _____

_____

_____

_____

5. _____

_____

_____

_____

6. _____

_____

_____

_____

7. _____

   _____

   _____

   _____

8. _____

   _____

   _____

   _____

Now that you've named the parts of speech, can you identify them in a sentence? In each of the following sentences write what part of speech it is below each word. Use *N* for noun, *P* for pronoun, *V* for verb, *ADJ* for adjective, *ADV* for adverb, *PR* for preposition, C for conjunction and *I* for interjection. This is tricky, but don't get discouraged.

1. Rose and Lionel always went to the store on Saturday.

   _____

2. They wanted to buy some comic books with their money.

   _____

3. "Yikes!" cried Lionel. "*X-Men* is on sale."

   _____

4. I love *X-Men*, but *Spawn* is definitely a great comic.

_____

5. *Spawn* and *X-Men* are both excellent.

_____

Chapter 2
The Sentence

Now that you know the parts of speech, let's talk about how sentences are put together. The parts of speech play different roles in different sentences. There are two main parts of a sentence. They are the **subject** and the **predicate.**

Why should you care about this? That's simple: because there must be a subject and a predicate in a complete sentence. Look at the following examples.

Not a sentence: John and Mary

Not a sentence: Went to the store

A sentence: John and Mary went to the store.

But do you always speak in complete sentences? No way! There are plenty of times when, for creative purposes, you may use only a fragment, or a piece of a sentence, to make your point. But if you are using fragments when you should be using full, complete sentences (in formal writing, for example), you will find yourself in hot water.

THE SUBJECT

If your friend asked you what the subject of the book
you were reading was, you'd tell her what the book
was about, right? Well, the subject of a sentence is
simply what the sentence is about. The easiest way to
find the subject of a sentence is to find the verb
(action word), and then ask yourself who or what is
doing that action. For example, look at this sentence.

> Bob ran in the race.

What is the verb? *Ran*. Who ran? Bob. *Bob* is the
subject of the sentence.

Not all subjects come first in a sentence.

> After running in the race, Eileen
> was exhausted.

What is the verb? *Was exhausted*. Who was
exhausted? *Eileen*. *Eileen* is the subject of the sentence.

Some sentences have more than one subject. Check
out this one.

> While Mike was painting, Grace
> was writing her paper.

There are two actions in this sentence—painting
and writing. Who was painting? *Mike*. *Mike* is the
subject of the first half of the sentence. Who was
writing? *Grace*. *Grace* is the subject of the second half.

There is *always* a subject in a sentence. Sometimes,
however, you don't hear or see the subject. These
subjects are *implied*. What does it mean to imply
something? It means that you don't say it straight

out, but it's what you mean. Saying "I guess you didn't study for this exam," is a teacher's way of implying that you didn't do that well, right?

So what is an implied subject? Look at this example.

> Get out of here!

This sentence is a complete thought. And how do you figure out the subject? Well, just as before, ask yourself these questions. What is the verb? *Get out.* Who is supposed to get out? Well, sorry, but you are. The subject here is *you.* In other words, the speaker is implying this.

> *You* get out of here!

Sometimes, then, when a speaker is directing a comment right at someone, he won't say *you* but *you* is implied. Here are more examples of an implied subject.

> Turn off the television.

> Don't eat that ice cream.

> Wait until 4:30.

✍ QUIZ #9 ✍
Subjects

Underline the subject in each of the following sentences.

1. Amanda stormed into the room.
2. "Get away from my boyfriend!"
3. "He is not your boyfriend!"
4. Amanda picked up a teddy bear and threw it at Jennifer.
5. Without a moment's hesitation, Jennifer ran out of the room.

Sometimes there are words between the subject and the verb; don't let these throw you off. For example:

> Mary, the best student in class, was awarded the blue ribbon.

Who was awarded? Mary—so Mary is the subject. The phrase "the best student in class" describes Mary.

Now look at the following sentence.

> One of the boys was going to give the speech.

This is a little trickier. Who is giving the speech? Not boys, but *one of the boys*. *One* is the subject. When you are looking for the subject, try to ignore the words that are describing it. Look for the verb and ask yourself who or what is performing the action.

Sometimes subjects consist of more than one word. Not all of the words are equally important. The simple subject is the most important word in a subject. It is usually a noun or a pronoun. The complete subject includes the simple subject and all of that words that modify it.

Sometimes the subject is modified by adjectives. Look at the sentence below.

The hyper young cat ran around the house.

Who ran around the house? The cat. The words *hyper* and *young* are modifying the word *cat*. The simple subject is *cat*. The complete subject is *The hyper young cat*.

✍ QUIZ #10 ✍
Springfield, Here We Come!

In the following passage, underline each verb and circle the complete subject that goes with it.

Thump. The clubhouse landed back in Babette's yard.

"I am glad we got to be cartoons," Sondra said. "I sure did like that feeling."

"Well, we have had a very exciting day so far, but we have been somewhat unlucky in our choices," Barnaby said.

"Listen, guys, you just don't know how to pick fun places," Bridget said. She blew a huge bubble and was lifted off the ground a few inches. "Why don't we visit the Simpsons in Springfield? We will have fun there. Bart is a riot. Maggie is so cute. Give me that ticket."

"Great! We can be cartoon characters again," Sondra said.

Bridget rubbed the ticket while humming the theme song to *The Simpsons*. The clubhouse began to shake once more.

THE PREDICATE

What is the predicate? It includes the verb in the sentence and the words related to it that complete the sentence's thought. It's the part of the sentence that tells more about the subject. It describes what the subject does or has. It can also tell what the subject is like.

The complete predicate includes all the words in the predicate of a sentence. The simple predicate is the main word in the predicate. It is always a verb.

The easiest way to find the predicate is to do your subject search (Where's the verb? Who or what is the verb talking about?). The verb and (usually) the rest of the sentence is the predicate. Take a look at some simple examples.

Subject	Predicate
Jake	was a man.
He	was nice to everybody.

Don't think, because of our simple examples, that the subject always comes first, and that the predicate always comes second. That's probably the easiest way to write sentences, but it would be boring if all sentences were constructed this way.

Sentences should be varied in good writing. That means that some sentences will be long and intricate, while others will be short and simple. Varying sentences in this way makes a piece of writing far more interesting to read. Let's look at a more complicated sentence and find the subject and the predicate.

> Throughout the history of the school, thousands of kids have walked these halls.

The verb of this sentence is *have walked.* Who or what *have walked? Thousands of kids.* So *thousands of kids* is the subject of the sentence. And what is the predicate? *Throughout the history of the school . . . have walked these halls.*

Now take a look at this one.

> There are a million reasons to eat candy.

First of all, remember that *there* is never the subject of a sentence; if you see *there* at the beginning, the subject will probably follow the verb. So what is the verb? *Are.* There are *a million reasons. A million reasons* is the subject. Therefore, *There are . . . to eat candy is the predicate.*

Who's Trespassing in Springfield?

Underline the complete subject and put parentheses around the complete predicate in each of the following sentences.

The water began to bubble up around their feet. The clubhouse was barely floating.

"We've landed in a swimming pool!" Bridget wailed. "What are we going to do?"

"Well, we should probably get out of this clubhouse pronto," Barnaby suggested.

Jennifer peered out the window. "I don't think that is a very good idea, Barnaby."

"Why would you say that, Jennifer? We happen to be sinking."

"Yeah, well I think I would rather drown." Jennifer pointed out the window.

"It's Chief Wiggum and the Springfield Police!" Bridget yelled.

"What are you kids doing in the Simpsons' swimming pool?" Chief Wiggum bellowed on a bullhorn. "All right, you kids come out with your hands up."

"*Anna banana!*" they all yelled at once.

Subject and Predicate Review

• Every sentence has a subject and a predicate.

• To find the subject

  Locate the verb.

Ask yourself "who or what is the verb talking about?"
That "who or what" is the subject.

- The predicate is the verb and all words related to it. The predicate may be a simple verb, or it may be the verb and all the extra things that are talking about the subject.

✍ QUIZ #12 ✍
Complete Sentences

Mark the complete sentences with an "S."
Mark the fragments with an "F."

___ 1. Granny marched into the room.

___ 2. After looking at the time, left to find Jed.

___ 3. Sniffling and crying in the corner.

___ 4. Elly Mae was a mess.

___ 5. Jethro couldn't help but notice what a mess Elly Mae was.

There are two more terms you need to know before moving on to the more complicated points of grammar. The terms are *phrases* and *clauses*.

PHRASES

A phrase is a group of words that cannot stand alone as a sentence. The words in a phrase work together as a part of speech. For example, they may work together to name a person, place, thing, or idea. In this case the group of words would be called a **noun phrase.** The two most common phrases, however, are the **prepositional phrase** and the **verbal phrase.**

Prepositional Phrases

Remember prepositions? They're those little words that locate a noun in time, space, or direction. Prepositional phrases always begin with a preposition and end with a noun. For example

> around the house
>
> *preposition   noun*
>
> through the door
>
> *preposition   noun*
>
> behind the wall
>
> *preposition   noun*

These are all prepositional phrases. Now you have to decide what part of speech these phrases are acting as by looking at how they work in the sentence.

> The black cat was buried *behind the wall.*

Go through your steps one by one.

1. What is the verb? *was buried*
2. What was buried? *The black cat. The black cat* is the subject of the sentence.
3. What does the prepositional phrase tell you? Where the black cat was buried. *Behind the wall* is a prepositional phrase that acts as an adverb in this sentence. It describes the verb *was buried.*

Here's one more example.

> *Before school* is the best time to take a shower.

1. What is the verb? *is*

2. When is? *Before school.* In this sentence, the prepositional phrase is the subject of the sentence. Because the subject of a sentence is always a noun, the prepositional phrase here acts as a noun.

Prepositional phrases *usually* act as adverbs or adjectives. When in doubt, ask yourself what the phrase is telling you in the sentence. When you are picking apart sentences for class or homework, it is usually helpful to put parentheses around prepositional phrases. They always work together and sometimes are distracting when you are trying to locate a subject and verb. For example:

> One of the boys in the group of a million is going to join us.

Now that's a long and complicated sentence. But you can gather the prepositional phrases like this.

> One (of the boys) (in the group) (of a million) is going to join us.

It may be clearer for you to see the verb (*is going*) and the subject (*one*). If you feel confused, try the following quiz. It will probably clear up the structure of a sentence for you.

Prepositional Phrases

Find the prepositional phrase or phrases in each sentence. Put parentheses around them.

1. At the house, Sydney put some ice on her nose.
2. Jake, who was in the kitchen, asked her if she wanted some soda.
3. Amanda, Sydney, and Jake were pretty shaken up after the incident.
4. As always, Amanda felt triumphant in her apartment.
5. Back at the pool, Billy was getting ready for a swim.

Verbal Phrases

Verbal phrases look like verbs. They have verbs in them, but they are not verbs. They act as nouns, adjectives, or adverbs. We will talk more about verbal phrases on pages 89–90.

CLAUSES

A clause is a group of words that includes a subject and a verb. There are two types of clauses: dependent and independent. An **independent clause,** which is also called a **principal clause,** makes sense standing alone. A **dependent clause** is used like an adjective, adverb, or noun. It depends on the other clause in the sentence to make sense.

> Billy told us that he would come to the party.

This is a sentence that is made up of two separate clauses.

> Billy told us that he would come to
> *clause 1*   *clause 2*
> the party.

Both of these clauses have subjects and verbs. But the first clause, *Billy told us,* is the independent clause, or principal clause in the sentence, because it can stand alone. *That he would come to the party* is the dependent clause. It wouldn't make sense by itself, and the words work together to modify the verb *told* in the independent clause. Billy told us *what*? *That he would come to the party.*

✍ QUIZ #14 ✍
Phrases and Clauses

Each of the following sentences contains one or two clauses. Underline the dependent clauses and put parentheses around the independent clauses.

1. After the party, Alison called Jane.
2. Unless you were there, you wouldn't believe it!
3. Jane called her sister before she found out.

4. Sydney told Jake about the incident.

5. When he returned, Billy spoke to Amanda.

Phrases and Clauses Review

- A **phrase** is a group of words that does not have a subject and a verb.

- The words in a phrase work together as a part of speech.

- A **prepositional phrase** always begins with a preposition and ends with a noun.

- A **clause** is a group of words with a subject and a verb.

- A **dependent clause** cannot stand alone as a sentence.

- An **independent clause** makes sense by itself.

SIMPLE, COMPOUND, AND COMPLEX SENTENCES

Some sentences are long and complicated, while others are short and simple. When you first learned to write, you probably wrote in short sentences. But that got boring after a while. Look at this paragraph.

> We went to the game. We sat in the sun. It was hot. We ate hot dogs. They were delicious.

Compare it to this one.

> We went to the game. We sat in the
> sun and it was hot. The hot dogs we
> ate were delicious.

As you get better at writing, you will want to
include some compound and complex sentences.
Read on.

Simple Sentences

A simple sentence is made up of one clause. It can
have more than one noun in the subject, or more than
one word in the predicate, but it can still be simple.

> Apples are my favorite.
>
> Apple and cherry are my favorite pies.
>
> Apples make delicious cider or pie.
>
> I like eating and drinking things
> made from apples.

In all of these examples, you cannot separate the
sentences into two or more clauses.

Compound Sentences

A compound sentence is made up of two or more
independent clauses (or simple sentences) that are
joined together with a conjunction. For example:

> We hiked to the picnic grounds and
> we ate our lunches.
>
> The movie was wonderful *and* I
> would see it again.

Zippy would eat fruit, *but* he hated vegetables.

Would you like to eat vegetables *or* would you rather have candy?

To decide if a sentence is compound, try to divide it into two or more complete sentences. If you can, then the sentence is compound.

Complex Sentences

A complex sentence has at least one independent clause and at least one dependent clause. You could break the sentence apart, and each part would have a subject and a verb, but at least one of the parts wouldn't make sense alone.

Iggy went to the store *where he bought JuJu fruits.*

He was convinced *that JuJu fruits were as good as real fruit.*

As you can see, the clauses in regular type could stand alone as sentences. The italicized clauses could not.

You may have noticed that a series of simple sentences can be turned into compound or complex sentences, depending on how you connect them. By the same token, if your compound or complex sentences begin to get too compound or complex, it may be easier to break them into smaller, simple sentences. Sometimes you can take a long dependent clause and turn it into a simple adjective.

Martha lives in a house, <u>which is
made of bricks</u>.

Martha lives in a brick house.

Both of these sentences are correct, but the second
one certainly sounds better. Some sentences sound
better when they are long and interesting, and some
sound better when they are short and simple. Mix
them up. Be creative. Reread your sentences to make
sure they sound good. Work on developing your
"ear" for good grammar and good style.

✍ QUIZ #15 ✍
Compound Sentences

**Rewrite each of these simple sentences as
one compound sentence.**

1. Amanda came home. She found Billy on her
   couch.

   _____

   _____

2. Billy told her to cool out. He would leave.

   _____

   _____

3. I want to cool out! She won't let me!

   _____

   _____

4. He ate pizza. It was his favorite food.

   _____

   _____

5. He ate it every day. It was fattening.

   _____

   _____

6. He ate the pizza. She ate brownies.

   _____

   _____

Now turn the following complicated, confusing sentences into one or two simple sentences.

7. JuJu fruits, which are red, are the most nutritious.

   _____

   _____

8. If you are going to San Francisco, which can be very foggy, make sure you bring your flashlight.

   _____

   _____

9. Eating hot dogs can be great, but Maria ate fifteen every day for lunch and soon began to feel sick about the whole thing.

_____

_____

_____

Sentence Review

- A **simple sentence** has one independent clause—a subject and a verb.

- A **compound sentence** has two or more independent clauses joined together with a conjunction. If you take it apart, the two clauses will make sense as separate sentences.

- A **complex sentence** has at least one independent clause and at least one dependent clause.

✍ QUIZ #16 ✍
Putting It All Together

In the following sentences, circle the verbs and underline the subjects. Also, mark "S" if it is a simple sentence, "C" if it is a compound sentence, and "X" if it is a complex sentence.

___ 1. Jennifer asked Sondra what it was that she wanted.

___ 2. I need help!

___ 3. Barnaby and Sondra offered to buy Bridget some fresh bubble gum.

___ 4. Do you think this ticket is so bad, even though we've had some misadventures?

___ 5. After she thought about it, Bridget was convinced that her friends were right.

___ 6. We've had some problems, but I still think this could be fun.

___ 7. Let's go!

___ 8. We will be together.

___ 9. We've had some bad luck, but we will try again.

One Last Note . . .

Okay, you've gotten through the first half of the book. In the second half, you're going to hear a lot more terms, and it may be confusing at first. Just remember the basics, and never hesitate to turn back and review something. All the terms you've learned are also in the glossary in the back of the book, so remember to check there as well.

Chapter 3
More About Nouns

In Chapters 1 and 2 of this book, we reviewed each of the basic parts of speech and the main parts and types of sentences. There's a lot more to know about each of these things, however. In Chapters 3, 4, and 5 we will focus on each of the parts of speech in detail and give you some extra grammar tips as well.

This chapter is devoted to different types of nouns and all of the rules that come with using them. As you may know, teachers can ask about strange-sounding things like "collective nouns" and "reflexive pronouns." Don't let the names of these things put you off. We're going to explain them here, too, so you will know what they are.

As you practice grammar and develop your "ear," you will find that you use many of these things naturally in your speech. Speaking and writing properly takes practice. Work on one or two things at a time so you can master each one.

TYPES OF NOUNS

You know that a noun is a person, place, thing, or idea, right? Now you can change a noun to show different things. For example, you can show that there is more than one thing by making the noun plural. Or you can show that a noun "owns" something by making it possessive.

Singular and Plural Nouns

If you have one of something, you use a **singular noun** to refer to it. If you have two or more of those things, you use the **plural** form of the noun.

> If you build a second *house*, you have two *houses*.

> If you find a second *mouse*, you don't have two *mouses*!

You have two *mice*. Your life would be so much easier if you had simple grammar rules to follow. There are some pretty consistent rules you can follow to show possession. There will always be exceptions, and we'll try to cover as many of them as possible. But first, let's go over the rules.

- You can make most words plural just by adding an -*s* at the end. For example:

alien/aliens	helicopter/helicopters
pizza/pizzas	book/books
joy/joys	soda/sodas
day/days	pickle/pickles
word/words	

- If a word ends in -*s*, -*x*, -*z*, -*sh*, or -*ch*, then you must add -*es*.

  Why? Because it sounds better. Those words need a different plural ending, or the plural would just run into the word. For example, we say *box-es* not *boxs*. Add the -*es* ending when you hear yourself adding a whole new syllable at the end.

box/boxes	Jones/Joneses
tax/taxes	dress/dresses
lunch/lunches	waltz/waltzes
fox/foxes	mess/messes
wish/wishes	

- If a word ends in *f* or *fe*, change the ending to a *v* then add -*es*.

  Why? Well, it also just sounds better. And, lucky you, it's another rule to remember.

calf/calves	knife/knives
loaf/loaves	elf/elves
leaf/leaves	shelf/shelves
half/halves	life/lives
thief/thieves	

- For words that end in *y*, change the *y* to *i* and add -*es* if the *y* comes after a consonant. If the *y* comes after a vowel, just add *s*.

baby/ babies	lady/ ladies
penny/pennies	monkey/monkeys
toy/toys	story/stories

• The weird ones.

Sometimes there are no rules! Some nouns change completely, and some don't change at all when they go from singular to plural. What do you do? If you are ever unsure about a plural noun, look it up. In the dictionary, any unusual plurals are listed right after the singular form of the word. Here are a few.

child/children   moose/moose
sheep/sheep   deer/deer
mouse/mice   woman/women
foot/feet   person/people
tooth/teeth

✍ QUIZ #17 ✍
Singular and Plural Nouns

Change the singular nouns in parentheses to plural nouns.

1. Sondra asked Jennifer to eat fifteen (banana)
   _____ .

2. Taylor told me that his twelve (monkey)
   _____ escaped from their (cage)
   _____ and wanted to wash their
   (foot) _____ in the bath.

3. My favorite (movie) _____ are
   (comedy) _____ .

4. If you are going to put (fox) _____ in
    (box) _____, you'd better not bring
    them to (church) _____ or feed them
    (lunch) _____.

5. The shoemaker's (elf) _____ put the
    (shoe) _____ on the (shelf)
    _____ all by themselves.

6. One of the great (joy) _____ of
    eating (burger) _____ is that you
    don't need (knife) _____.

7. "Do you know where the (lady)
    _____ who sold me these (shoe)
    _____ are?" asked Babette.

8. "I believe they are hiding in the (bush)
    _____ or behind that group of
    (man) _____," Taylor replied.

9. If you clear the (dish)
    _____ from the
    table, make sure you
    wrap the (leftover)
    _____ and put
    the (bowl)
    _____ in the
    refrigerator.

10. If you take out the (paint)
    _____, wash the
    (paintbrush) _____
    before you use them.

Collective Nouns

A **collective noun** is a noun that refers to a group of people who usually act together. Because of this, the noun is almost always treated as singular. If there is more than one group of people, the noun is plural. Some examples of collective nouns are *audience, jury, family, government,* and *class.*

Look at the following sentences.

> The seventh-grade *class* went to Washington, D.C.

(The noun is singular because it refers to one group that is acting together.)

> The seventh- and eighth-grade classes went to the museum.

(The noun is plural because it refers to two groups acting together.)

Possessive Nouns

If a person, place, or thing "owns" something, you can use a **possessive noun.** It will make your sentences sound much more smooth and clear. For example, instead of

> the coat *of Bert*

> the sweater *of Ernie*

> a vacation *of a week*

you can say

> ***Bert's*** coat
>
> ***Ernie's*** sweater
>
> a ***week's*** vacation

As you know, a noun is either singular or plural. That will affect how you make it into a possessive.

- If a noun is singular, always add -'s, even if it ends in s. For example:

Bert	Bert's hat
Charles	Charles's homework
dress	dress's hemline
girl	girl's house
James	James's bicycle

Okay, we admit that *James's* looks a little odd. And, to be honest, if you wrote *James'* that would be okay too. But to be safe and to keep your rules as simple as possible, remember that all singular nouns get -'s at the end when made possessive.

- If a noun is plural but that it doesn't end in s, add -'s. If it does end in s, just add the apostrophe. Let's take a look.

babies	babies' room
children	children's room
ladies	ladies' room
men	men's room

To summarize, just add -'s to any noun to show that it is possessive unless it is a plural noun ending in s. Then, simply add the apostrophe.

✍ QUIZ #18 ✍
Possessives

Fill in the missing parts of the following chart.

Singular	Singular Possessive	Plural	Plural Possessive
berry			
cat			
desk			
dog			
family			
glove			
house			
Jones			
peach			
thief			

Direct and Indirect Objects

Remember that in order to find the subject of a sentence, ask yourself what the verb is, and then what is performing that action. That's the subject. The **direct object** of the sentence is the receiver of the action. Let's start with a simple sentence.

Bozo threw confetti.

What's the verb? *Threw*. Who threw? *Bozo*. *Bozo* is the subject of the sentence. He does the throwing. What is getting thrown? *Confetti*. So, *confetti* is the direct object of the sentence.

You must have a direct object before you can have an **indirect object.** If we give you more information about this event (Bozo threw the audience confetti), *the audience* is the indirect object. It tells you "to whom" or "for whom" the action was being done. You can always spot an indirect object by pulling it out and making a prepositional phrase with it. In this case, you might have said

Bozo threw confetti (at the audience).

Look at this one.

Zelda gave Zorba a fancy jacket.

Zelda is the subject. What is the direct object and what is the indirect object of the verb *gave*? What did she give? *A fancy jacket*. That is the direct object. *Zorba* is the indirect object. You can check by making it into a prepositional phrase.

Zelda gave a fancy jacket (to Zorba).

It is also worth remembering that if you have both a direct object and an indirect object, the indirect object usually comes between the verb and the direct object.

✍ QUIZ #19 ✍

Finding Direct and Indirect Objects

In each of the following sentences, circle the direct object and underline the indirect object (if one exists).

1. Dylan told Brenda the bad news.
2. Brenda sold Tiffani rights to the story.
3. The police asked Dylan several questions.
4. We wanted bananas and peeled grapes for the party.
5. Brandon ate ninety-eight bananas before winning the contest.

Predicate Nouns

One kind of noun you find in the predicate of a sentence is an object (direct or indirect.) But some verbs do not take objects. The most common example is the verb *to be* (*is, are, will, am,* etc.). The verb *to be* is like an equals sign. In this case, the noun in the predicate will rename or explain the subject. Other verbs that may take predicate nouns instead of direct objects are *to become, to seem,* and *to appear.* You can always tell a predicate noun or pronoun because it will be equal to the subject.

Krusty is my favorite clown.
(Krusty = clown, so *clown* is the predicate noun.)

Homer is a strange father.
(Homer = father, so *father* is the predicate noun.)

Springfield is the largest city in the state.
(Springfield = city, so *city* is the predicate noun.)

Not all sentences have predicate nouns. To determine whether if a noun is a predicate noun or a direct object, just ask yourself if it equals the subject.

Lisa plays the saxophone.
(Lisa = saxophone? No, so, *saxophone* is the direct object.)

Lisa is the lead in the play.
(Lisa = lead? Yes, so *lead* is the predicate noun.)

✍ QUIZ #20 ✑
Identifying Predicate Nouns

Underline the predicate nouns in the following sentences.

1. Bart is an intrepid explorer.
2. Always afraid of his shadow, Mr. Burns is a coward.

3. That kid with the glasses is Milhouse.
4. Maggie is the youngest child.
5. Homer seems like a new man.

PRONOUNS

Remember that a pronoun takes the place of a noun.

Personal Pronouns

Personal pronouns take on different forms depending on to whom they refer.

First person refers to the speaker: *I, me, mine, my, we, us, our, ours* are all the pronouns you would use if you were speaking in the first person (the speaker is talking about herself).

Second person refers to the person being spoken to: *you, your, yours* are second person pronouns. Use them when you are speaking directly to someone.

Third person refers to the person being spoken about: *he, him, his, she, her, hers, it, its, they, them, their, theirs* are used when you are talking about other people.

Formal Reports

Most teachers prefer you not to use the second person, *you*, in your written work, because it is the most informal of the personal pronouns. It is usually preferable to use the pronoun *one* instead of *you*. Check with your teacher if you are not sure. Here is an example. You can say

One will see the insect species I
have described in the picture below.

or

The insect species I have described
is shown in the picture below.

but not

You will see the insect species I
have described in the picture below.

Pronoun Case

There are two sets of personal pronouns—subject
pronouns and object pronouns. *Subject* pronouns are
referred to as the **nominative case.** *Object* pronouns
are referred to as the **objective case.**

Nominative (subject) Pronouns

Singular	Plural
I	we
you	you
he, she, it	they

Use a subject pronoun

• as the subject of a sentence. The subject is
the doer of the action described by the verb.

She threw the ball. (Who threw? *She*)

I went to the party. (Who went? *I*)

We wanted ice cream. (Who wanted? *We*)

They came to our store. (Who came?
They)

- after using a form of the verb *to be* (*am, is, are,* or *will,* for example). Remember, the verb *to be* is like an equals sign; anything after it will be the same form as is before it. If you have a subject noun before, you need a subject pronoun after. You can think of this as the "phone rule." It's the way you answer the phone—when someone calls and says "I'm looking for a Ms. Oakley," the person would answer, "This is she."

Objective (object) Pronouns

Singular	Plural
me	us
you	you
her, him, it	them

Use an object pronoun

- as the direct object of a verb. The subject of a verb is the doer of the action. The direct object of the verb is the receiver of the action.

> She asked *me* to come to the party. (Who did she ask? *Me.*)

> I picked *them.* (I picked what? *Them.*)

- as the indirect object of a verb. An indirect object tells to whom or for whom the action is being done.

> I picked *her* flowers.

> Marilyn gave *him* a punch in the nose.

- as the object of a preposition.

> I gave the flowers to *her*.

> We ran with *them* to the race.

Some Tips

One of the most common errors people make is to confuse the subject and object pronouns. There are a few common pitfalls you can avoid with practice.

- Say, "between you and me . . ."

  It's not "between you and I." The pronouns are the objects of the preposition *between* and are always in objective form. So it would be "between you and him," or "between me and him," or whatever pronouns you use.

- If you are making a comparison, complete the comparison in your head to decide if you need a subject or object pronoun.

> Sally is smarter than *I / me*.

  Finish the comparison: Sally is smarter than *I am*.

> She is as tall as *he / him*.

  Finish the comparison: She is as tall as *he is*.

  This rule may seem a little strange, so you should practice it.

- If you have a compound subject or predicate, try saying each one separately to figure it out.

Bob and *I/me* went to the store.

To check

Bob went to the store.

I went to the store.
Mary went with Paul and *him/he*.

To check

Mary went with Paul.

Mary went with *him*.

- What about . . .

    We/Us kids went on the hike last Saturday.

To check

    Take out *the kids: We* went on the hike last Saturday, so *we* is correct.

✍ QUIZ #21 ✍
Babette in the Big City

Underline the correct pronoun in each of the following sentences.

After returning from Springfield, Barnaby looked at Babette. (He, Him) wanted to know what (she, her) thought of that trip.

"Darling, that place was a dump, believe (I, me). New York City is a place where there's some real action. We can meet the cast of *Seinfeld:* Jerry, Elaine, Kramer, and George. That George is a cutie pie. Let (us, we) go there," Babette cried.

"Do you think (us, we) really should try again?" (they, them) all wondered aloud.

"(Us, we) will never know unless (us, we) try again!" Babette told (they, them).

"Between you and (I, me)," Jennifer whispered to Bridget, "(I, me) don't care if (I, me) ever see New York City."

"Give (I, me) the ticket, darling," Babette ordered. "Oh, George, (I, me) can't wait to meet you."

The clubhouse rumbled. Thwump! (They, Them) landed in Jerry's apartment.

"Who's there?" (they, them) heard a voice call from the kitchen.

Possessive Pronouns

You know that you need to add -'s to make a noun possessive. But with pronouns, it's a different story. Possessive pronouns do not take apostrophes at all. Take a look at the personal pronouns and their possessive forms.

Personal pronoun	Possessive form
I, me	my
you	your
he, him	his
she, her	hers
we, us	ours
they, them	theirs
it	its
who, whom	whose

There is no apostrophe in the possessive form of these pronouns. Don't confuse the possessive forms of some pronouns with similar contractions.

its (possessive form)	*it's* (contraction standing for *it is*)
whose (possessive form)	*who's* (contraction standing for *who is*)

Relative, Reflexive, Demonstrative, and Interrogative Pronouns

Okay, don't panic. These are actually pretty easy. Let's look at them one at a time.

Relative Pronouns

These pronouns link a relative clause to the main clause of a sentence. There are two types of relative pronouns: definite and indefinite. **Definite relative pronouns** stand for a definite noun. **Indefinite relative pronouns** are not preceded by a definite noun (also called an antecedent).

Definite Relative Pronouns	Indefinite Relative Pronouns
which	what
that	which
who	who
whom	whatever
	whom
	whomever

> Zelda went to see F. Scott, *who* was quite dashing in his white suit.

The main clause of this sentence is *Zelda went to see F. Scott. Who was quite dashing in his white suit* is a relative clause because it cannot stand alone. Here it modifies, or describes, F. Scott. The relative pronoun, *who*, links the two clauses.

The following are the rules for relative pronouns:

- If you are deciding between **who** and **whom,** just substitute *he* and *him*. If you would use *he*, then use *who*. If you would use *him*, then use *whom*.

- **Who** and **whom** refer to people.

- **That** can refer to people, animals, or things.

- **Which** cannot refer to people.

- **That** and **which** are commonly misused and confused. In general, *that* begins an adjective clause that is essential to the meaning of a sentence. *Which* introduces an adjective clause that is nonessential to the meaning of the sentence. *Which* generally follows a comma; *that* doesn't.

> I like apples *that* are green and tart. (The adjective clause is essential to the meaning of the sentence.)

> I like apples, *which* are very healthy and good to eat. (The adjective clause is nonessential to the sentence's meaning. It simply adds additional information.)

✍ QUIZ #22 ✍
Relative Pronoun Practice

Underline the correct relative pronoun in each of the following sentences.

1. Sideshow Bob, (who, whom) is Krusty's faithful sidekick, was after Bart.

2. *The Krusty the Clown Show*, (which, that) is Lisa's favorite, is on at 4 P.M. each day.

3. The *Itchy and Scratchy* episode (which, that) Bart and Lisa like the best is quite gory.

4. Could these be the children (who, whom) I brought into the world?

5. Maggie's favorite pacifier is the one (that, which) makes the most noise.

Reflexive Pronouns

When you think of reflexive pronouns, think about reflections. These pronouns act like mirrors. They refer to the subject in the sentence. The reflexive pronouns are *myself, yourself, herself, himself, ourselves, yourselves, themselves, itself.* Check out the following rules:

- Make sure that the reflexive pronoun agrees with the noun it mirrors.

  They went around talking about *themselves.*

  David ate all fifty cookies by *himself.*

- You may use them for emphasis, but don't do it too often.

  > She won the championship *herself*.

  > I, *myself*, am quite proud of my accomplishment.

- Don't substitute reflexive pronouns for subject pronouns.

  > Paul and *I* went to the museum.

not

  > Paul and *myself* went to the museum.

Demonstrative Pronouns

A demonstrative pronoun demonstrates which noun in the sentence is being talked about. The demonstrative pronouns are *that, these, this*, and *those*. Here are the rules.

- A demonstrative pronoun must take the place of a specific noun. Otherwise, it is really just an adjective.

  > I want to drink all of **this**. (*This* refers to something the speaker is pointing to, such as milk or apple juice, so it is a demonstrative pronoun.)

  > This dress is new. (*This* is an adjective describing the *dress*. Which dress? This dress.)

Those are completely worthless!
(*Those* refers to things the speaker is talking about, so it is a demonstrative pronoun.)

Those books are completely worthless!
(*Those* is an adjective modifying *books*. Which books? Those books.)

- Remember, using demonstrative pronouns is not an excuse for being imprecise. You need to let your reader or listener know what it is you are referring to.

Interrogative Pronouns

As the name suggests, these pronouns are used to interrogate, or ask questions. The interrogative, or question pronouns, are *who, whom, which,* and *what.*

Who are you?

What do you want?

Which house do you live in?

Whom do you want to see?

Pronoun Agreement

While this is the last pronoun topic we are covering, it is one of the most important. When you use a pronoun, you must be sure that it agrees in number with the noun it replaces: Use a *singular* pronoun to replace a singular noun. Use a *plural* pronoun to replace a plural noun. For example:

Gilligan found *two coconuts* and ate *them* up.

Mary Ann put *her* new bathing suit on.

As with all rules, there are a few points to keep in mind.

The A NOSE Rule

As a rule, use singular pronouns to refer back to any of these words: anybody, anything, nobody, nothing, neither, one, someone, something, each, every, and either. You can remember them because they begin with the letters A, N, O, S, or E. For example:

The Professor felt that *everyone* should do *his* part on the island.

Neither Mary Ann nor Ginger felt *she* was going to be rescued.

As you can see, this rule may sometimes lead to awkward-sounding sentences. You might end up saying things like

Before *a boy or a girl* tries out for sports, *he* should practice.

Technically, that's correct. But realistically it sounds stupid and sexist. What happened to the girl? Should you say

Before a boy or a girl tries out for sports, *he or she* should practice.

Yikes! You're being even more awkward with that one. How about the following:

> Before a boy or a girl tries out for
> sports, *they* should practice.

We'll be honest—this is how most people handle it. But it's wrong! Sloppy! Don't fall for the "they trap." *They* has become an all-purpose pronoun used by people who can't dig themselves out of the grammar trap. What to do? When in doubt, *rewrite.* How about

> Before *boys and girls* try out for
> sports, *they* should practice.

By rewriting the whole sentence with a plural subject, you get to use the nice, easy plural pronoun *they.* You haven't offended anyone and your sentence is grammatically correct. Be consistent.

- Remember not to switch pronouns in a sentence.

> *You* must turn on *your* stereo before
> listening to *your* music.

not

> *One* must turn on *your* stereo before
> listening to *one's* music.

- Make the nouns that go with your pronouns consistent in number.

> *Each* of the boys asked for *a raise* in
> *his* allowance.

not

> *Each* of the boys asked for *raises* in
> *his* allowance.
> (Individual boys get one raise each.)

> *All* the students took *books* out of
> the library.

not

> *All* the students took *a book* out of
> the library.
> (If there's more than one student,
> there should be more than one
> book. Unless, of course, they were
> all taking out the same book.)

- Make sure your reader knows which noun
  you are referring to when you use a
  pronoun. Look at the following sentence.

> Mr. Howell and the Skipper were
> sure that *he* could get them off the
> island.

He who? Were they sure that Mr. Howell, with all
his money, could get them off the island? Or were
they sure that the Skipper, with his sailing expertise,
could get them off the island? You would have to say
the following if that's what you meant:

> Mr. Howell and the Skipper were
> sure that *the Skipper* could get them
> off the island.

✍ QUIZ #23 ✍

Pronoun Agreement

Cross out the incorrect pronoun in each sentence and replace it with a better one.

1. Either Ginger or Mary Ann was sure to have brought their new bathing suit.

2. Anybody who has seen *Gilligan's Island* is certain to know that they have seen a classic.

3. "If anyone finds a way off this island, would they please let us know?" cried Mr. Howell.

4. "Oh, Thurston," called Mrs. Howell, "neither Gilligan nor you is able to figure out what they really want."

5. "All of them are happy as clams to be here. We want to stay on this island forever!" cried Mary Ann.

Chapter 4
More About Verbs

Verbs are the very heart of a sentence. They express action or states of being. Without a verb, you cannot have a sentence. So, you might say that verbs are the most important part of a sentence. There's a lot to do here, so let's get started.

TYPES OF VERBS

Subject-Verb Agreement

You must make sure that the subject and verb agree in number: *Singular* subjects take *singular* verbs. *Plural* subjects take *plural* verbs.

How simple could life be? How do you recognize a singular and a plural verb? Well, in general, you add -*s* to a noun to make it *plural,* and add -*s* to a verb to make it *singular.* Strange, but true. Check it out.

Singular	Plural
The girl jumps.	The girls jump.
The kitten frolics.	The kittens frolic.
The fat lady sings.	The fat ladies sing.
The shark swims.	The sharks swim.

Of course, this isn't true for all verbs, but it is true for most of them. In general, you must first check the subject; then ask yourself if the subject is singular or plural. Then make sure the verbs match.

> *Greg and Cindy were* afraid of the ghost that haunted the attic.

> *My sister*, the silly one, *was* sick of figs.

Don't be fooled by a group of words that may separate the subject and the verb. Remember to bracket off the prepositional phrases—they are never part of the subject.

> The *bunch* (of kids) (in the yard) *is* going to sing a song.

> *One* (of the several thousand) (in the state) *was* going to make it to the semi-finals.

Subject-Verb Tips

- Bracket off prepositional phrases—they are never part of the subject.

- Locate the verb. Ask yourself who or what is doing the action.

- Locate the subject.

- The subject and the verb should match. Plural subjects take plural verbs, and singular subjects take singular verbs.

- Subjects joined by *and* are plural. Subjects joined by *or* are singular.

> Jan *or* Cindy *is* going to win.

> Greg *and* Bobby *are* the best swimmers around.

✍ QUIZ #24 ✎
Subject-Verb Agreement

Match the correct verb with the subject in the following sentences. Underline each correct verb.

1. Alice (cook, cooks) for the kids every night.

2. Every night, she (make, makes) their favorite meal: meatloaf.

3. "(Wasn't, weren't) we going to have something different tonight, Alice?" (ask, asks) Cindy.

4. "Yikes! Meatloaf again!" (cries, cry) Jan and Marcia. "We need some variety!"

5. "(Doesn't, don't) you people have anything better to do than worry about dinner?" (wonder, wonders) Alice.

6. "Oh, no, not meatloaf!" (yell, yells) Mr. Brady from upstairs.

7. "Oh, I (am, is) sick of trying to please all of you finicky Bradys!" Alice says as she (stomp, stomps) out of the house for the last time.

Tenses

Verbs not only tell you what happened, they tell you *when* it happened. The "when" part is called the verb **tense.** There are three main tenses: past, present, and future.

Past Tense

This is the tense you use whenever you are talking or writing about something that has already happened.

> Yesterday, I *fell* down.

> An hour ago, I *went* to the store.

> Once upon a time, a beautiful princess *was born.*

Anytime the action takes place in the past, whether it was an hour ago or a thousand years ago, you use the past tense. Most stories are written in the past tense—it is the easiest and most natural way to tell a story.

✍ QUIZ #25 ✍

Mr. Brady! Save Us from George!

Change all the present tense verbs that don't make sense to the past tense. Rewrite the passage in the space provided after it.

George comes into Jerry's living room and sees the clubhouse. The kids are shaking when they hear him yell and scream. "This clubhouse! Why is it landing in Jerry's apartment?"

Babette looks out of the window. "What a hunk!" she cries. "But he is being so violent. I am scared."

"Get out of here, or I'll call the police."

"Quick, give me the ticket. I have an idea," Taylor says. He rubs the ticket and cries, "Help us, Mr. Brady!"

Suddenly, Mr. Brady walks into the apartment. "Hey!" he yells, "stop hitting that clubhouse!"

George turns around. "This is my friend's apartment. I'm watching it for him, so I'll hit whatever I want."

"Excuse me, kids, but who lives here?"

"His friend does," Babette points sheepishly toward George.

"Sorry, bud. My mistake." Mr. Brady picks up a golf club and waves it at the clubhouse with George. "Okay, you kids, get out of here or I'll have to call the police."

"*Anna banana!*" Taylor throws his hands up in disgust.

Rewrite the passage with past tense verbs on the lines below.

_____

_____

_____

_____

_____

_____

_____

_____

_____

_____

_____

Present Tense

This is the tense you use to show that something is happening right now.

> I *am* here.

> Right now, I *am listening* to my best friend.

It can also be used to show something you do all the time.

> Every day at three o'clock, I *run* to the track for practice.

> I *take* a shower every morning.

You should use the present tense when you are stating a fact or an opinion.

> Metallica *is* the best band around.

Future Tense

This is the tense that is used to show what is going to happen.

> Tomorrow, I *will go* to the Red Hot Chili Peppers show.
>
> In an hour, I *will run* in the race.
>
> Next year, I *will be* in high school.

There are more than three tenses; in fact, there are twelve altogether. Before we talk about how the different tenses are formed, we must discuss the principal parts of the verb.

Principal Parts

Three forms of a verb are the most important—they are used to form the different tenses. They are called the principal parts of the verb: the **present tense,** the **past tense,** and the **past participle.**

Regular Verbs

A regular verb is a verb in which the principal parts are all formed the same way—the past tense and past participle are formed by adding *-ed, -d,* or *-t* to the present tense. For example:

Present	Past	Past Participle
ask	asked	asked
climb	climbed	climbed
dive	dived	dived
drag	dragged	dragged
drown	drowned	drowned
sneak	sneaked	sneaked

The Perfect Tenses

Use the **present perfect** if

- the action started in the past and continues to the present.

> I *have sneaked* two miles so far. (I am still *sneaking*.)

- the action started in the past and was finished at an earlier time.

> I *have sneaked* 150 miles in my spy-training routine so far.

Use the **past perfect** if

- you want to show one thing that happened in the past, before something else that happened in the past.

> Before I sneaked to his house, I *had sneaked* to three other houses.

Use the **future perfect** if

- you want to show an action that will be completed at some future time. (This is a rarely used tense.)

> By next Tuesday, I *will have sneaked* around the whole neighborhood.

Tenses Tip

Four of the tenses have words that tip you off to them.

> **Future:** *shall* or *will*
>
> **Present perfect:** *has* or *have*
>
> **Past perfect:** *had*
>
> **Future perfect:** *shall have* or *will have*

Helping Verbs

You may have noticed that many sentences have verbs that are more than one word long. Verbs may be two or three words long, as you can see in the future perfect tense. In the following example, there is a main verb and one or two helping verbs.

> He *will have eaten* all my favorite cookies by next week.

Here, *will have* is the helping verb for the main verb, *eaten*.

Tenses

Fill in the correct verb form in each blank. The verb is in the infinitive form at the end of each sentence.

1. Yesterday, Barnaby _____ twenty-seven chocolate chip cookies. (to eat)

2. Before he finished the cookies, he _____ four dozen. (to bake)

3. Right now, Bridget _____ her favorite bubble gum. (to chew)

4. Tomorrow, Barnaby and Bridget _____ to Jennifer's house. (to go)

5. By next Wednesday, Barnaby _____ another thirty batches of chocolate chip cookies. (to bake)

6. Mr. James said that he _____ the budget for WNYX next month. (to cut)

7. Dave and Lisa's productivity _____ after they stopped dating. (to drop)

8. Johnny Johnson was sent to jail after he _____ to take over Jimmy's empire. (to threaten)

9. After wondering why everyone was giggling at him all day, Beth _____ Matthew that someone had taped the word "Spaz" to the back of his sweater. (to tell)

10. Joe _____ crazy gadgets out of duct tape and clay in his spare time. (to build)

Irregular Verbs

Irregular verbs are verbs that do not follow the standard formula for making past tense verbs and past participles. Some irregular verbs are so common that you don't really have to think about them. *To be* is a commonly used irregular verb: I *am*, I *was*, I *have been*, I *will have been*.

Principal Parts of Some Irregular Verbs

Present	Past	Past participle
blow	blew	blown
bring	brought (not brang)	brought
creep	crept	crept
draw	drew	drawn
drink	drank	drunk
freeze	froze	frozen
get	got	got, gotten
grow	grew	grown
hang	hung	hung (I hung a picture.)
	hanged	hanged (The man was hanged.)

Present	Past	Past participle
lay	laid	laid (I laid the book down.)
lie	lay	lain (I have lain in bed.)
ring	rang	rung
shake	shook	shaken
shrink	shrank, shrunk	shrunk, shrunken
sink	sank	sunk
slay	slew	slain
spring	sprang, sprung	sprung
swear	swore	sworn
swim	swam	swum
tear	tore	torn
weep	wept	wept
wring	wrung	wrung

✍ QUIZ#27 ✍
Correct Verb Forms

Underline the correct form of the verb in each sentence.

1. Max (wept, weeped) when he heard the bad news.

2. "My brother has (grew, grown)," he said.

3. "I have (laid, lain) on my bed too long!" she exclaimed.

4. "If I had (tore, torn) that piece of paper, no one would have found out."

5. "I (brang, brought) this on myself," thought Rosa.

6. Mr. McMahon (swore, sworn) that his daughter Stephanie would never marry a wrestler.

7. Kurt Angle (hanged, hung) his Olympic gold medals on his bedroom wall.

8. Many competitors have (froze, frozen) in fear at the sight of "Stone Cold" Steve Austin.

9. The match began when the timekeeper (rang, rung) the bell.

10. The Rock had been (shaken, shook) after the Undertaker hit him with a chair.

What Is Voice?

You may use two types of voices when you are writing—the active voice and the passive voice. The **active voice** is when the subject is performing the action. The **passive voice** is when the action happens to the subject. For example:

Active: Michael drove the car.

Passive: The car was driven by Michael.

As you can imagine, it is preferable to use the active voice when you are writing. It is almost always the clearer way to say something. When you use the passive voice, you usually write a muddled, confused sentence.

Here are a few more examples.

Active: We attended the concert.

Passive: The concert was attended by us.

Active: Cats purr to indicate contentment.

Passive: Purring indicates contentment for cats.

Verbals

A verbal is one of three types of phrases—participles, gerunds, and infinitives—that looks like a verb, but acts like a noun, adjective, or adverb.

Participles

It looks like a verb, but it isn't a verb. Think of a participle as a verb that acts like an adjective in a sentence. Look at the difference.

I *had fallen* down the stairs.

The leaf, *fallen* from the tree, was quite beautiful.

In the first sentence, *had fallen* is the verb. In the second, the past participle *fallen* is used by itself as an adjective to describe the leaf.

Here are a couple more examples.

I *had known* that he would be famous one day.

Known for his great laugh, Billy was famous.

In the first sentence, *had known* is the main verb in the sentence. *Known* in the second sentence is used to help describe Billy; it is an adjective.

✍ QUIZ #28 ✍
Find the Participles

Put parentheses around the participles in the following sentences.

1. When he discovered his missing barbecued ribs, Vince called for Linda.

2. Christian used the peaches picked from the tree to bake a pie.

3. Mr. Austin thought that Shane's answer was wrong because it included a misspelled word.

4. It is a great convenience to have running water.

5. There were so many screaming children in the movie.

Gerunds

While participles are verbals that are used as adjectives, gerunds are verbals that are used as nouns. Gerunds are easy to spot: they are verbs ending in *-ing*. For example:

> *Skating* is my favorite thing to do.

Skating is a noun, and here it acts as the subject of the sentence.

Here's another example.

> *Collecting* stamps is Edwina's favorite hobby.

Collecting is not a verb in this sentence; it is a noun. *Collecting stamps* is the subject of the verb *is*.

✍ QUIZ #29 ✍
Spotting Gerunds

Underline the gerunds in each of the following sentences.

1. I always liked playing baseball.
2. We all enjoyed running out onto the field.
3. Batting is the one thing I don't do well.

4. Fielding is my area of expertise.

5. Winning, however, is something everybody likes.

Infinitives

Infinitives can act like nouns, adjectives, or adverbs. An infinitive is a verb form with the preposition *to*. If you see *to* with a noun, it's a prepositional phrase, but if you see to with a verb, it's an infinitive. The infinitives of the verb *help*, for example, are *to help, to have helped, to be helped,* and *to have been helped.*

Noun: A doctor hopes *to help* his patients.

Adjective: Which of these books would be the one *to help* me study? (*To help* modifies the noun *the one.*)

Adverb: My sister told us stories *to help* pass the time. (*To help* modifies the verb *told.*)

✍ QUIZ #30 ✍
Infinitives

Underline the infinitive in each of the following sentences.

1. Jethro wanted to see the sights in Beverly Hills.

2. To go to the races was Granny's favorite pastime.

3. Mr. Drysdale wanted to eat with the Clampetts.

4. Elly Mae hoped to win the beauty contest that week.

5. Milhouse always has to run from Jimbo after school.

6. Ralph waits until the teacher is out of the room before he starts to eat paste.

7. "To work at the DMV is no picnic," Patty said to Selma.

Chapter 5

More About Adjectives, Adverbs, Prepositions, and Other Details

ADJECTIVES AND ADVERBS

What Are the Comparative Forms?

Using the right adjective is easy if you know the rules. Most adjectives have three forms: the positive, the comparative, and the superlative. Use the **positive form** when you are talking about one thing, the **comparative form** when you are comparing two things, and the **superlative form** when you are comparing more than two things.

Positive: The berry is *sweet.*

Comparative: The blueberry is *sweeter* than the strawberry.

(comparing two things)

Superlative: The raspberry is the *sweetest* berry of all.

(comparing more than two things)

The Comparative and the Superlative

If an adjective has only *one* syllable, add -*er* for the comparative form, and -*est* for the superlative form. If the last letter is -*y*, change the *y* to an *i*.

Positive	Comparative	Superlative
slow	slower	slowest
fast	faster	fastest
dry	drier	driest

When an adjective has *two* syllables things get a little trickier. Sometimes you will add -*er* for the comparative form and -*est* for the superlative form. At other times you will add *more* for the comparative form and *most* for the superlative form. If you are not sure, check the dictionary. It will suggest which comparative and superlative forms to use.

Positive	Comparative	Superlative
silly	sillier	silliest
funny	funnier	funniest
graceful	more graceful	most graceful

If an adjective has three or more syllables, add *more* for the comparative form and *most* for the superlative form.

Positive	Comparative	Superlative
ridiculous	more ridiculous	most ridiculous
argumentative	more argumentative	most argumentative

Some adjectives have irregular comparative and superlative forms. Check out the following examples.

Positive	Comparative	Superlative
bad	worse	worst
good	better	best
little	less	least
many	more	most

For example:

Positive: Jane is friendly.

Comparative: Peter is *less* friendly than Jane.

Superlative: Nancy is the *least* friendly of everyone in the class.

However, some adjectives never take a comparative or superlative form because they express something that is perfect or complete. In other words they cannot be more or less. For example:

unique
perfect
infinite
dead

Something cannot be more unique or less perfect. If you really need to modify these adjectives, you should use adverbs, such as nearly, almost, or hardly, to show that something approaches these qualities.

nearly perfect

almost dead

hardly unique

Finally, you should always avoid using double comparisons such as *more uglier, most friendliest.* Use either *uglier* or *friendliest* instead.

✍ QUIZ #31 ✌

Comparative Forms of Adjectives

Underline the correct adjective form in the following sentences.

1. Of all the kids, Barnaby was the (smarter, smartest).

2. Taylor was (quieter, quietest) than Jennifer.

3. Instead of yummy mashed potatoes or healthy string beans, Bridget likes bubble gum (better, best).

4. Between Sondra and Taylor, Sondra is the (odder, oddest) person.

5. Babette is the (more, most) mysterious person you have ever met.

Using the Correct Adverb/Adjective

Adverbs and adjectives are commonly confused, because they often sound very similar. If you are unsure if a word is an adverb or an adjective, look it up. Keep in mind that many adverbs end in -ly. But, most important, remember that adverbs modify verbs, adjectives, and other adverbs, while adjectives modify nouns. Look at the following sentences.

> Mary went *quick/quickly* up the stairs.
> (Use *quickly*, the adverb, because you are describing the verb, *went*.)

> She sure is a *quick/quickly* runner.
> (Use *quick* because you are describing the noun, *runner*.)

The Good/Well Confusion

Good and *well* are words that everybody mixes up. How often have you heard, "I just know you'll do good on that test"? That's wrong. Remember that *good* is an adjective and *well* is an adverb. If you are talking about how you will "do," then you need to modify it with an adverb. Check out the following examples.

> That song is *good*. You play it *well*.

> This meatloaf is *good*. You cook so *well*.

Well can also be an adjective. When it means "in good health" or "attractive." So, it is correct to say

> You look *well*.

> I feel *well*.

Adjectives and Adverbs

Underline the correct words in each of the following sentences.

1. Amanda felt (good, well) on that (beautiful, beautifully) day.
2. Jake wanted (bad, badly) to call her and tell her how (sad, sadly) he felt.
3. Sydney told her sister that she dressed (good, well) for such a (good, well) day.
4. After coming to a (sudden, suddenly) stop, Jake's (new, newly) sports car screeched (loud, loudly).
5. Stomping (forceful, forcefully) out of the room, Amanda flipped her (thick, thickly) blonde hair out of her (cool, coolly) eyes.

MODIFIERS AND PREPOSITIONS
Misplaced Modifiers

> Driving down the lonely road, my mind wandered and I veered off into a ditch.

Do you know what's wrong with this sentence? It may sound just fine, but look closely at the opening phrase, "Driving down the lonely road." Who or what was driving down the lonely road? Well, it sounds like "my mind" was driving, because that's the closest thing to the modifying phrase.

- The rule for modifiers is simple: Place the modifier as close as possible to the thing it modifies.

Why? This makes a sentence clear and precise. If you carelessly move modifiers all around your sentences, you will confuse your readers. For example:

> While eating chocolate chip cookies, the front door blew open.

Now, who or what was eating chocolate chip cookies? The front door? The front door is the subject of the sentence. If you want to be clear that *you* were eating the chocolate chip cookies, and not some scary front door, change the sentence around.

> While I was eating chocolate chip cookies, the front door blew open.

or

> While eating chocolate chip cookies, I saw the front door blow open.

Here's another example.

> After finishing the race, my shoes stank.

Again, who or what finished the race? My shoes? That doesn't make sense. So change it to

> After I finished the race, my shoes stank.

How could you make the following sentence more clear?

> To make a model rocket, hard work and precision is required.

Try the following.

> To make a model rocket, you must work hard and use precision.

What about single-word adjectives and adverbs? Look at these two sentences.

> He only voted for David for class president. (meaning he didn't help with the campaign)

> He voted only for David for class president. (meaning he didn't vote for anyone else)

What about this sentence?

> Do you ever remember seeing such a wonderful U2 concert?

or

> Do you remember ever seeing such a wonderful U2 concert?

If you're modifying the verb seeing, put the adverb *ever* before and as close to the verb as possible. The second sentence probably comes closer to the writer's intended meaning.

Misplaced Modifiers

**Underline the misplaced modifier, and then
rewrite each of the following sentences.**

1. Approaching his favorite TV star, admiration
   was oozing out of Barnaby.

   _____

   _____

   _____

2. Hearing the voice of Wilma, a wave of
   excitement came over Sondra.

   _____

   _____

   _____

3. Going to the set of the TV show *Friends*, the
   ride was bumpy for Babette.

   _____

   _____

   _____

4. Thinking about Rachel, a pole was walked
   into by a dreamy Jennifer.

   _____

   _____

   _____

Using the Correct Preposition

It is not always easy to pick the correct preposition. While there are few rules concerning the correct use of prepositions, unfortunately there are hundreds of idioms that use prepositions. (An idiom is just an expression that doesn't mean exactly what it says.) Here are some examples of the more easily confused prepositions.

at, by

Use *by* only when you mean *past* or *by way of.*

> We went *by* school on our way to the concert.

> He stopped *at* the store after school. (not *by the store*)

at, to

Use *to* for motion. When you go to a place, you are *at* it.

> Margot and I were *at* the mall all afternoon.

> We are going *to* the movies later.

at, with

Use *at* for a thing, and *with* for a person.

> I was furious *with* my mother for not allowing me to go to the mall.

> I was angry *at* the new rule at school that doesn't allow us to leave campus.

between, among

Use *between* when you have two things, and *among* for more than two things.

> *Between* you and me, this is the worst party I have been to this year.

> *Among* the fifteen parties I have gone to, this is by far the worst.

> *Between* the English department and the social studies department, there are very few good teachers.

(Note: Even though there are more than two people in the English department and the Social Studies department, you are talking about two groups, so you should use *between*.)

beside, besides

Beside means *next to*. *Besides* means *in addition to*.

> I want to sit *beside* Jimmy tonight.

> I hope you'll talk to someone *besides* him.

from, off

Don't use *off* when you mean *from*. *Off of* is never correct.

> I bought the Janet Jackson CD *from* my favorite store.

> Get *off* the bus at Fourth Street to get to my house.

over, to

You cannot go *over* someone's house unless you have wings. Use the preposition *to*.

> We went *to* Marcel's new beach house last summer.

> Batgirl flew *over* our heads.

Idiomatic Prepositional Phrases Which Will Impress Your Friends

Do you need to memorize these? Nope. Just read through them to see if there are any you usually use incorrectly. Try to work on them. You may also use this list as a reference when you write.

angry *about* (an idea, a thing): Babette was *angry about* the ridiculous situation in which she was involved.

angry *with* (a person): Babette was *angry with* Simone for causing it.

compare *to* (shows similarity): *Compared to* the *Mona Lisa,* this is a really good painting.

compare *with* (shows similarity and difference): You can't *compare* that *with* the *Mona Lisa!*

decide *on* (use with a noun): Let's *decide on* a movie.

decide *to* (use with a verb): Let's *decide to* eat out.

differ *with* (means to disagree): I *differ with* Mr. Pinkley regarding that Shakespearean sonnet.

differ *from* (means unlike): Mittens *differ from* hats because you wear mittens on your hands.

fail *in* (an attempt): I *failed in* my efforts to win first prize.

fail *to* (do something): Jeannette *failed to* submit her paper on time.

practice *for/to* (use when practice is a verb): I am *practicing for* the track meet. I have to *practice to* do well.

practice *of* (use when practice is a noun): The *practice of* cheating is not condoned by our school.

result *from/in* (when result is a verb): Weak fingernails *result from* not eating well. Not eating well *results in* weak fingernails.

result *of* (when result is a noun): This is the *result of* not eating well.

sympathy *for* (means to feel for): Brian had *sympathy for* Matt.

sympathy *with* (means agreement, sharing of feelings): Matt had *sympathy with* Brian's position in the matter.

Don't Use Prepositions With These, Please . . .

continue: I will continue my project. Not: I will continue with my project.

inside: Paul is inside the pet house. Not: Paul is inside of the pet house.

meet: I want to meet the exchange student. Not: I want to meet with the exchange student.

name: Edwina was named best brain. Not: Edwina was named as best brain.

off: I fell off the homecoming float. Not: I fell off of the homecoming float.

visit: I am going to visit Amy this spring. Not: I am going to visit with Amy this spring.

If you are unsure, try to eliminate the extra preposition. If the sentence makes sense without it, you probably don't need it.

What about ending a sentence with a preposition? You may have already heard this rule. You should try to make sure your sentences don't end with a preposition—prepositions always take an object noun, so if you don't have one after the open preposition, it is sort of left dangling there. You can correct this by rewording your sentence

> I didn't know which house Marlene lived *in*.

to

> I didn't know *in* which house Marlene lived.

This is one of those rules that isn't strictly followed. If you are writing a formal school report and you absolutely don't want to have a single error, you probably should think about this rule. However, if it sounds too stiff and awkward to reword your sentences when you are speaking, go ahead and leave the preposition at the end. It's not really a big deal.

QUIZ #34
Preposition Time

Underline the correct preposition in each of the following sentences.

1. Tom went (to, by) Michael's Pet Store yesterday.

2. You know, Tom is really very different (from, with) Michael.

3. When Tom bought that fish (off of, from) Michael, we were all very surprised.

4. (Beside, Besides) Tom, Michael doesn't have many friends.

5. (Between, Among) Michael and Tom, Tom is more friendly.

6. Tom was upset (at, with) Michael for selling him such a boring pet.

OTHER DETAILS ABOUT GRAMMAR
Faulty Comparison

When you are comparing things, you must be sure to compare nouns to nouns and verbs to verbs. Take a look at the following sentence.

Michelle loves Marcel more than me.

Now, what's the problem? We're comparing Michelle's love of Marcel with . . . what? That's the problem—it isn't entirely clear. Does Michelle love

Marcel more than she loves the speaker here? Or, does Michelle love Marcel more than the speaker loves Marcel? In matters of grammar, as in matters of romance, you must be perfectly clear at all times. The speaker here should say either

> Michelle loves Marcel more than I do.

or

> Michelle loves Marcel more than
> she loves me.

Here's another example.

> Oranges are much more wonderful
> to eat than apples.

Sounds fine, right? Well, this is one of those sentences that is pretty clear, but not really because the rules of grammar have been broken. In this sentence, we are comparing *eating oranges* with *apples.* We want to compare *eating* with *eating*, so we should have said

> Oranges are much more wonderful
> to eat than apples are.

Finally, remember that comparisons almost always use *like, as, than,* or *unlike.* If you use any of these words, make sure you are making a good, solid comparison.

✍ QUIZ #35 ✍
Faulty Comparisons

Correct the error in each of the following sentences.

1. "I love Mary Ann's smile so much more than Ginger!" cried Barnaby.

   _____

   _____

   _____

2. "That may be true, but the storyline on *Friends* is far better than *Gilligan's Island*," shrieked Jennifer.

   _____

   _____

   _____

3. "The storyline may be better, but Rachel's character is not nearly as nice as Mary Ann," answered Babette.

   _____

   _____

   _____

4. "Rachel's dresses are far more stylish than Mary Ann," offered Taylor.

   _____

   _____

   _____

5. "Perhaps, but I still think that Mary Ann's hair is much prettier than Rachel," whispered Barnaby.

_____

_____

_____

Parallel Construction

If you are listing a series of things, you should make sure that they are all similar in form. For example, you may have a series of nouns.

> After going to many different movies, Ziggy realized that *character*, *style*, and *plot* were all equally important.

However, the sentence below is incorrect.

> After going to many different movies, Ziggy realized that *character*, *style*, and *if there was a good plot* were all equally important.

Do you see how the final part of the list, *plot*, was changed from a noun to a clause? If you start off listing nouns, make sure all the parts of your list are nouns.

You may have a series of phrases like the following:

> Paul hoped *to go* to college, *to get* a good job, *to go* to graduate school, and *to settle* down.

Look at the following sentence.

> Paul hoped *to go* to college, *to get* a good job, *to go* to graduate school, and *settling down*.

Do you hear how the direction changed at the end of that list in the sentence above? The first example is correct because everything on the list is in the same form. (They are all infinitive verbs.)

✍ QUIZ #36 ✍
Parallel Construction

Correct the error in each of the following sentences.

1. The castaways had tried many different ways to get off the island: building rafts, signaling with flares and to call ships with their radio.

   _____

   _____

   _____

2. Fred and Wilma were hosting the annual company picnic. They fried brontosaurus burgers, grilled stegosaurus ribs, and were barbecuing hot dogs as well.

   _____

   _____

   _____

3. Amanda wanted to be successful, make a lot of money, and building a great empire.

_____

_____

_____

4. Warning: Watching too much television can damage your brain, cause eye strain, and may be interfering with your ability to read.

_____

_____

_____

5. After eating, jumping rope, and to go swimming, the gang went back to the clubhouse.

_____

_____

_____

Chapter 6
Punctuation

What's the point of punctuation? Take a look at these two sentences.

> Martha, my mother is the best pilot around.

> Martha, my mother, is the best pilot around.

In the first sentence, I am telling someone named Martha about my mother. In the second sentence, I am telling someone about my mother, whose name is Martha. The words in each sentence are exactly the same. The punctuation changes the meaning of the sentence.

With punctuation there are certain rules, many of which are open to interpretation depending on your personal style. While you are learning, however, it's best not to fool around too much with long, strange, and overly punctuated sentences. Keeping sentences relatively short and simple will keep you out of the punctuation mud for now. As you get more adventurous and confident, you can try your hand at interesting sentences filled with dashes, semicolons, and commas.

THE PERIOD

Use a period in the following instances.

- When you are coming to a complete stop after a statement or a command.

  The garden around my house is very dense.
  Elvis Presley was the greatest performer ever.

- After most abbreviations. Monograms, government organizations, television and radio networks, and post office state abbreviations *don't* need periods. If you have an abbreviation at the end of a sentence, you only need one period. Look at the examples below.

  Mr. Panda V.P. Cheney etc. A.M.

  CBS WBCI KZOO FBI JFK

- Inside parentheses if they contain a complete sentence. Put the period outside the parentheses if the words inside do not make a complete sentence.

  (Mary told him.)

  Mary told him (not us).

- Inside quotation marks at the end of a sentence.

> The sign said "Authorized Personnel Only."

- After all the letters and numbers for an outline, unless they are in parentheses.

I.

  A.

  B.

II.

  A.

  B.

    1.

    2.

    3.

THE COMMA

Use a comma

- to separate two independent clauses connected by *and, but, or, nor,* and *for.*

> Pierre was usually a good runner, but today he lost the race.

> Tom was a good cook, and he always
> enjoyed eating what he made.

If the clauses are short enough, you may leave out the comma.

> Pierre won and he was happy.
> Tom cooked and ate the fish.

- to separate items in a list. You should also put a comma before the last *and*.

> I wanted to buy the new CDs by
> Madonna, Prince, and REM.

- to set off an introductory phrase from the main sentence.

> After eating fifty-two lemon pies, Billy
> had quite a bad stomachache.
> Before leaving the party, Billy had to
> take some Alka-Seltzer.

- to separate a list of adjectives if you could use *and* between them.

> The fat, sickly, ugly, smelly baboon was
> sitting in the corner.
> (You could say "The fat and sickly and
> ugly and smelly baboon . . .".)

- to separate the name of a person you are addressing, or a person's title.

> That is why, Mr. Smithers, Dagwood
> won't be at work today.
> Mr. Smithers, Dagwood's boss, is quite
> upset about the budget.

- to set off a group of words that contrast with what you are saying.

> I like to swim, not dive, when I go to the pool.
>
> Alice was going to sing, not dance, at the talent show.

- to set apart the figures in a date and the parts of an address (however, not between the state and the zip code.)

> July 4, 1776
>
> 35 Elm Street, Cleveland, OH 00001

- to separate hundreds, thousands, millions, and every three digits thereafter.

> 1,876,967,300

- to avoid confusion in a sentence. That's the main purpose of a comma, after all. If you need to pause, or set aside a group of words to make your meaning clear, use a comma. Try not to overdo it.

> After waking up, my sister ate breakfast.

The next sentence is confusing without a comma.

> After waking up my sister ate breakfast.

THE QUESTION MARK

Use a question mark as follows:

- To show that a direct question is being asked.

> Do you want to go to Michael's Pet Store with me?

You don't need a question mark for an indirect question.

> She wanted to know if he would be going to the pet store with her.

- Put the question mark inside quotation marks if the quotation is a question. Put the question mark outside the quotation marks if the quote itself is not a question.

> "Would you like some of this fish?"
> (The quote is a question.)
> Do you know who said, "Give me liberty or give me death"?
> (The quote is not a question.)

THE EXCLAMATION POINT

Use an exclamation point

- if you are expressing a strong statement or sentiment.

    I really love that movie!

- to set off an interjection for emphasis.

    Yikes! That fire is hot.

But don't overuse exclamation points. People use them way too much. Try to limit the use of exclamation points to strong feelings and statements, or your writing will look silly. Take a look at these two examples.

> The Pineview Eagles have been having their best year ever! Star quarterback David Barzinski did a great job this past Saturday! He scored two touchdowns! It was a great game! Go, Eagles!

or

> The Pineview Eagles have been having their best year ever. Star quarterback David Barzinski did a great job this past Saturday. He scored two touchdowns. It was a great game. Go, Eagles!

The first example seems as if the writer is yelling. It also loses its effectiveness after awhile. Try to keep your use of exclamation points to a minimum, and never use two or more in the same place.

THE SEMICOLON

Semicolons are tricky, and many people don't use them correctly. Here are the rules.

- Use a semicolon when two independent clauses are not joined by a conjunction. If you can separate the parts into two separate sentences, use a semicolon.

> Marlene felt that the fish was overcooked; the dinner was wonderful other than that.
>
> The results came in; Georgette was the clear leader.

- Use a semicolon if you have a long list of names that already includes commas. In this case commas would not clearly separate the names, so use semicolons instead.

> We were soon joined by Prof. Elizabeth Young-Smith, head of the English department, from Middle Valley, Ohio; Dean Jane Farfetch, team leader, from West Hills, Indiana; and Ms. Petra Mustang, social studies teacher, from South Eastville, Michigan.

THE COLON

A colon is used

- to introduce a list.

     The problems were always the same on the island: floods, volcanoes, and monsoons.

- to introduce a long quote.

     It was John F. Kennedy who said: "Ask not what your country can do for you; ask what you can do for your country."

- to introduce an explanation.

     There are many reasons for our coming here: we wanted to meet Michael, and we were interested in purchasing a new pet.

QUOTATION MARKS

Use quotation marks

- around a direct quote. Put any commas or periods inside the quotation marks. Question marks and exclamation marks should be inside the quotation marks only if they are part of the quote or outside if they are not.

     "Let's get going," said Jane "or we'll be late."

     "Don't you want to go?" asked Chris.

     "Look at me!" cried Barnaby.

     I don't think Mr. Smith knows we call him "Mr. Evil"!

- to set off a statement that is the opposite of what you really mean. Only use quotation marks this way if it is absolutely necessary, or your writing will look silly.

> Michelle "borrowed" my homework so that she could copy it.

- if a quotation is longer than one paragraph. Use new quotation marks at the beginning of each new paragraph, but only at the end of the last paragraph.

> "I went to the beach one day this summer. It was quite beautiful and sunny. The day was really picture perfect.
>
> "Then, to my surprise, a giant thundercloud passed over the sun. It began to rain. The day was completely ruined."

However, there is one exception to the quotation marks rule.

- You don't need quotation marks for an indirect quote.

> He told us that he would be happy to join us at the party.
>
> She said thank you to all her guests.

THE DASH

Dashes are optional. Some people love to use dashes—others don't.

- You may wish to use dashes like commas, to set off a phrase.

> She was quite a sight—all done up and wearing that new dress—for her sweet sixteen party.

- You may substitute dashes for parentheses.

> When you come to the party—it's going to be crowded—bring lots of tortilla chips and guacamole.

Instead of

> When you come to the party (it's going to be crowded) bring lots of tortilla chips and guacamole.

PARENTHESES

Parentheses are used as follows:

- To set off any extra words that would otherwise interrupt your sentence.

> Max (wonder dog extraordinaire) was performing at the local talent show.

✍ QUIZ #37 ✎
Anna Banana, We're Home!

Punctuate the following passage. Remember that there is some flexibility here, but do your best and try to keep the passage clear. Rewrite the passage in the space provided after it.

Barnaby Babette Sondra Taylor and Jennifer were all quite tired but exhilarated nonetheless

The Professor was not quite as smart as I'd always hoped but it was neat to finally see him anyway Barnaby said

Maybe you're right about the Professor said Jennifer but no one could compare to Rachel and her amazing clothes

Are you kidding She was so mean said Taylor

I think we all had some pretty exciting adventures said Jennifer but I for one am happy to be back here All that fighting and drama has worn me out

Yes agreed Taylor I don't think I would really want to be in The Brady Bunch after all

I would definitely not want to be a part of that stupid *Seinfeld* show said Babette I am very glad to be home

The gang soon realized one thing being part of a television show would be pretty exhausting after a while

Let's burn that ticket said Taylor It's the only safe reasonable thing to do

I think he is right said Barnaby Logically speaking of course we should cut our losses and just hang here despite the great heat

They made a ceremonial fire and watched the silver ticket crumple and burn

There's no place like home cried Bridget

Rewrite the passage with correct punctuation on the lines below.

_____

_____

_____

_____

_____

_____

_____

_____

_____

_____

_____

_____

_____

_____

_____

_____

Chapter 7

The Princeton Review List of Commonly Misused and Confused Words

LEARNING TO SPELL CORRECTLY

Some people are naturally good spellers. To a degree that's true. Some people have a knack for spotting misspelled words. Good spelling is not just about memorizing rules and words; it's a matter of recognizing words. In fact, good spelling often means learning to spot a misspelled word—not necessarily knowing how to spell every word.

Does that seem strange? Good spellers don't automatically know how to spell everything, but they do recognize words that are misspelled. To them, misspellings just look funny. How do you cultivate this talent? There are two steps.

1. **Reading is probably the best way to train yourself to recognize misspelled words.** Why? The more you look at words that are spelled correctly (and let's assume that in most books the words are spelled correctly), the more you recognize incorrectly spelled words. It's like eating in good restaurants all the time—after a while, you start to know the difference between good food and bad food.

2. **Edit your own work.** Before you hand in your work, get in the habit of rereading your work before you hand it in. Circle or mark any words that look even slightly wrong to you. How many can you spot? If you are using a computer, try to check for misspellings before you use the spell checker. It would be really great if you looked up all those words, but right now, the first step is to train yourself to recognize words that look wrong.

Now What?

Soon, you'll notice which words you always misspell. It's just a bad habit. Do you have some rule in your head like "*i* before *e* except after *c*" and as a result you always spell weird incorrectly as wierd? That's understandable. You should look at the words you misspell and think up a mnemonic to remember how to spell them.

What's a Mnemonic?

A **mnemonic** (ni MAHN ik) is a little memory device. A spelling mnemonic is "*i* before *e* except after *c*." But there are other ways to remember the correct spellings of words.

Look at the part of the word you always misspell. For example, sep*e*rate is a common misspelling. Now look at the right way to spell that word: sep*a*rate. Check out the spot in the word that gives you trouble. Almost everybody puts an *e* instead of an *a* in the middle. In order to remember the correct spelling, you may say to yourself: "There's *a rat* in separate."

And what about weird? You may just remember that *weird* is, well, a weird word, so it doesn't follow the rules.

What If I Can't Think of a Mnemonic?

If you really can't think up a mnemonic, we're willing to bet you memorized the spelling of the word just by thinking about it so hard. Many times it helps to sound out the word **phonetically** (pronounce the word in your head exactly the way it is spelled) if it has a strange spelling. For example, you might say the phrase *to get her* to yourself whenever you spell *together.*

Don't Use Silly Spellings When You Write!

We have to put a plea in for this—don't write using fun, silly spellings of words such as *nite* (instead of night), *thru* (instead of through) or, most important, *luv* (instead of love). These may be okay for notes to your friends, but you should never use them in any formal writing assignment.

Commonly Misspelled Words

achievement	*i* before *e* except after *c*
believe	*i* before *e* except after *c*
committee	2 *m*'s, 2 *t*'s, 2 *e*'s
definite	no *a*—just 2 *i*'s
occasion	2 *c*'s, but only one *s*
occurred	2 *c*'s, 2 *r*'s
parallel	There are 2 parallel *l*'s in the middle.
pleasant	There's an *-ant* in pleasant.
receive	*i* before *e*, except after *c*
recommend	one *c*, 2 *m*'s
referring	only one *f*
separate	There's *a rat* in separate.

DICTION

Diction means word choice to fit a certain context. Using the right word at the right time not only shows how brilliantly you speak and write, but it makes your speaking and writing clearer and more precise. If you use the wrong word, people will think your speech or writing is sloppy, or they may misunderstand your meaning. The following list of words are among those most commonly misused. You hear many of them used incorrectly every day.

The Offending Words

Absolutely

Do you mean *yes?* If you're writing, better to use the simpler, more direct word.

Affect/Effect

Affect is a verb. It means *to influence.* You can *affect* a situation in which you are involved. Your teacher can *affect* your grade in English. Your mother can *affect* your ideas about life.

Effect is usually a noun, meaning result. The *effect* was stunning. The special *effect* in the movie was spectacular.

Effect can sometimes be used as a verb as well—if it is, it means *to accomplish.* The new principal hoped to *effect* a number of changes in the school.

Aggravate/Irritate

You *aggravate* a situation. You *irritate* a person. *Aggravate* means to *make something worse.* If your mother tells you that you're *aggravating* her, you can tell her that, no, in fact, you are *irritating* her. Won't that do the trick? Tommy was *irritated* by his aunt's frequent nagging about his hair. The skin rash was *aggravated* by the lotion.

Agree to/Agree with

You *agree to* something and *with* someone. Helen *agreed with* John. They *agreed to* stop fighting for just one day.

Ain't

Ain't no such word. Always use *isn't* instead. There *isn't* any reason for you to do poorly on the test.

Allusion/Illusion

When you refer to something indirectly, that's an *allusion*. An *illusion* is that rabbit out of a hat trick. Her speech was sprinkled with *allusions* to all the famous people she had met. Making the Statue of Liberty disappear was one of David Copperfield's greatest *illusions*.

Alot/A lot

You say *a little*, right? Why should *a lot* be made into one word? There is no such word as *alot*. She had *a lot* of reasons not to do her homework.

All together/Altogether

All together means *together as a group*. *Altogether* means *completely*. We were *all together* this year for Thanksgiving. You are *altogether* right about that one!

Among/Between

Use *among* when you are talking about more than two things. Use *between* only when referring to two things. If you have two groups, you may also use *between*, even though there may be a lot of people in each group. The slimy fight *between* the citizens of Butterville and Margarinetown continued for many years. *Between* you and me, that was the worst fish I've ever eaten. *Among* the students in Ms. Ella's class, Ida Mae was the best.

As/Like

Use *as* when you are comparing phrases, and *like* when you are comparing nouns and pronouns. She's almost as smart *as* I am. He's just *like* his brother.

Basically

Avoid this word whenever you can. It's not technically wrong, but it is overused. Often you don't need it at all. Instead of "Basically, I'm in it for the money," you can just say, "I'm in it for the money."

Being that/Being as

These sound pretentious. Remember that the point is to be clear and precise. Just say *because*. *Because* I want to do well, I am avoiding silly-sounding phrases.

Beside/Besides

Beside means *next to*. *Besides* means *in addition to*. Try not to mix them up. "I was hoping to sit *beside* Jake," Sydney said. You have a lot to worry about *besides* Amanda.

Between you and . . . ?

Okay, once and for all: the correct phrase is *between you and me*, not between you and I. Remember that *between* is a preposition, so it always takes an object pronoun. *Between you and me*, this is the most delicious slop I've ever eaten.

Bring/Take

You *bring* things to the person who is speaking. You *take* things away from the person who is speaking. *Bring* me the head of Caesar! "*Take* this tray to your mother," said Dad. "*Bring* me the tray!" yelled Mom.

Borrow/Lend

Same idea as above: you *borrow* from someone; you *lend* to someone. May I *borrow* your book? I'll *lend* it to you.

Can/May
People almost always use *can* when they mean *may*.
Asking if you *can* leave the room is asking if you have
the ability to leave the room. Use *can* if you want to
know if you are able to do something. Use *may* if you
want to ask for permission. "*Can* I eat 280 cherry
pies?" wondered Beatrice. "*May* I watch her try?"
asked Beatrice's sister, Lilly.

Can't hardly
Hardly is a negative word. If you can't hardly, then
you can. What you want to say is *can hardly*. The
same is true for *can barely*. I *can barely* keep my eyes
open. I *can hardly* wait for my birthday.

Compare/Contrast
You *compare* things when you think about their
similarities and differences. If you are *contrasting*
things, you are only looking at how they are different
from each other. The teacher asked us to *compare* the
characters in the books we are reading. The *contrast*
between Ms. Hoffmeyer and Mr. Zinger is striking—
she is so laid back and he is so tense!

Compare with/Compare to
Compare with is generally used when you have two
equal things and you want to point out differences.
Compare to is used to point out similarities. *Compared
with* Mr. Wylie's class, Ms. Smith's is a breeze! Shall I
compare thee to a summer's day?

Complement/Compliment
To *complement* with an *e* means to go together with. To
compliment with an *i* means to say nice things about.
You can remember the difference by thinking that I

like to receive *compliments*. Spaghetti *complements* meatballs so perfectly. Mr. Smyth *complimented* my use of perfect grammar.

Could of

It's always wrong. The right thing to say is *could have*. The same holds true for would of or should of. I *could have* been a contender!

Further/Farther

Farther refers to time and quantity measurements. Use *further* to mean *more*. He couldn't go any *farther* on the trail after he sprained his ankle. Laurice wanted to have *further* discussion about the new rules.

Fewer/Less

Fewer refers to things that can be counted. *Less* refers to a general quantity. This one's fun, because you can catch many teachers asking for "five pages or *less*," when they should be asking for "five pages or *fewer*." How about those express lines at the supermarket? How many signs can you spot that say "ten items or *less*"? (That's wrong!) I'd like *fewer* french fries and *less* mashed potatoes. Give me *fewer* egg rolls and *less* soup.

Former/Latter

Former refers to the first of two things and *latter* refers to the second, or last of the two. You can remember these because *former* begins with an "*f*" just like first and *latter* begins with an "*l*" just like last. Money and health: the *former* can make you comfortable, but only the *latter* can make you feel good.

Goes

Do you mean *says*? If you say things like, "So, she goes, 'Get outta here!'" then stop it! Don't say *goes* unless you are talking about someone going somewhere. If you are telling someone what someone else said, use the right word, *says*. Mary Ann *says*, "Get out of my face!"

Healthful/Healthy

If you lead a *healthful* life, you will be *healthy*. *Healthful* refers to something that gives you health or leads to good health. People, plants, and animals can be *healthy*. Diet, climates, and exercise programs can be *healthful*. I stopped eating potato chips and now I feel so *healthy*. But my new *healthful* life is just no fun.

Hopefully

People misuse this word all the time. *Hopefully* means *with hope*. For example, you wait *hopefully* for the results of your test (meaning that you are waiting with hope). Technically you shouldn't say "Hopefully, we will come here tomorrow" unless you mean that you will all come here tomorrow "with hope." The easy way out of this is to use *I hope* when you are writing: *I hope* to do well on my exam. *Hopefully* is so widely misused that it is becoming acceptable, especially in speech.

Imply/Infer

If you *imply* something, you are hinting at it. You *infer* something when you figure it out. If your father *implies* that you need a haircut, you might infer that he doesn't like your style. Mr. Katzenjammer *implied* that we would have a pop quiz tomorrow. Marjorie *inferred* from Joe's nervous behavior that he liked her.

Immigrate/Emigrate

To *immigrate* is to move to a new country. You *emigrate* from the country you are leaving. Think of the *immigrants*—they were coming to the United States. The *immigrants* of the early 1900s came to Ellis Island. They *emigrated* from Ireland during the great Potato Famine.

In regards to

Use *regarding* or *in regard to* (no s). *Regarding* your letter, I will be there on the 14th.

Intelligent/Intelligible

Intelligent means smart. If something is *intelligible*, it is understandable. Lionel's speech was *intelligent*; he made references to all the books in our course. Rose's speech was *intelligible*; she spoke clearly and loudly.

Irregardless

No such word. Say *regardless*. *Regardless* of what you think, I am going to dye my hair green.

It's/Its

It's is a contraction meaning *it is*. We know it's confusing, but *its* is the possessive form of the pronoun *it*. Remember that none of the possessive pronouns take -'s. Think of his, hers, theirs, ours—none of them have an -'s. *It's* so difficult to keep all these chairs straight. That chair is broken; *its* leg is cracked in the middle.

Lay/Lie
These are confusing. Check out the section on weird verbs (page 86–87). *Lay* means to set down. *Lie* means to recline. *Lay* the book on the table. *Lie* on the couch.

Many/Much
Same as fewer/less. Use *many* for things that can be counted and *much* for a general quantity. *Many* of the people at the party were pigs. *Much* of the dip was gone by the time I got to the buffet table.

Most
Be careful not to use this word when you mean *almost*. Don't say, "*Most* everyone was there." *Almost* everyone was there.

Nauseated/Nauseous
Most people say *nauseous* when they mean *nauseated*. If you are *nauseous,* you make someone sick. If you are *nauseated,* you feel sick. If something is *nauseous,* it makes you *nauseated*. The smell of rotten eggs is *nauseous*. She was *nauseated* by the idea of eating the pet fish.

Number/Amount
Same as fewer/less. *Number* refers to things that can be counted. *Amount* refers to a quantity of things that cannot be counted separately. I have a *number* of dollars in my wallet. The *amount* of money she spends is mind-blowing! The *number* of eggs in the recipe was reduced. The *amount* of milk was increased.

Persecuted/Prosecuted

If you *persecute* someone you annoy them excessively. To *prosecute* means *to be brought before a court of law.* I think Mr. Van Dam is trying to *persecute* me with all this homework! This country believes that criminals should be *prosecuted* for their crimes.

Principle/Principal

The *principal* of your school is your pal—it ends in *pal.* Principal also functions as an adjective meaning most important. A *principle* is a rule or a guideline. The *principal* reason *Principal* Green was there was to help out. His *principles* inspire him to help people.

Respectively/Respectfully

Respectively means *in that order. Respectfully* means *with respect.* Some people sign letters *respectfully* yours. The most important things in life are health, happiness, and money, *respectively.* I submit this application to you *respectfully.*

Snuck

No way! The correct past tense form of sneak is *sneaked:* She *sneaked* down the hall, past her sleeping parents, and off to the party.

Stationary/Stationery

Remember that *stationery* with an *e* goes into an envelope (which starts with *e*) and is sold in a *stationery* store. *Stationary* with an *a* means staying still: The spider remained *stationary* for hours, waiting for its prey. Our local *stationery* store sells the prettiest blue *stationery.*

Too/To

Too is an adverb meaning *also* or *more than enough*. *To* is a preposition—use it to place a noun. We are going *to* my house after dinner. You are *too* much!

Ultimate

Use *ultimate* to mean *final*. Don't use ultimate to mean the best, as in the "ultimate taste sensation!" You'll sound like a commercial. They finally reached their *ultimate* destination—home.

You're/Your

People get this one wrong all the time. *You're* is a contraction meaning *you are*. *Your* is the possessive form of the pronoun *you*. *You're* invited to the party! *Your* puppy is so cute.

✍ QUIZ #38 ✍
Diction

Underline the correct word or words in each of the following sentences.

1. After returning from her adventures, Bridget was so tired, she was barely (intelligent, intelligible).

2. We need to buy some paper from the (stationary, stationery) store and write all this down.

3. ("Your, You're) kidding, right?" said Barnaby. "(Its, It's) (to, too) unbelievable."

4. "That stupid ticket sure was (aggravating, irritating). We hardly had (none, any) good luck," growled Jennifer.

5. "If we had (fewer, less) adventures, we wouldn't have anything fun to talk about," Sondra pointed out.

6. "We should have (snuck, sneaked) past George and gone to find Jerry," Babette pouted.

7. "Well, I am going to (lay, lie) down now and take a nap. That was exhausting," Barnaby said.

The School of Redundancy School

A redundancy occurs when you repeat yourself, or use words that are not necessary. The following phrases are redundant. Try to avoid using them.

4 A.M. in the morning—A.M. means in the morning. P.M. means *at night*. Don't say *9 P.M. at night* either.

At this point in time—Just say "at this time," or how about plain, old "now"?

An approximate guess—You either approximate or you guess. Same thing.

Believe you me—When you say "Believe me," the you is implied, so you don't need to include it.

Both alike—If you say simply "They are alike," you don't need to say "both."

Circle around—If you are circling, you are going around. Just use "circle."

Consensus of opinion—Just say consensus. If you have a consensus, you have a whole bunch of opinions working together. The *consensus* was that Mr. Geekly was the worst teacher in the school.

Dead corpse—A *corpse* is *dead.* But you knew that, didn't you?

Estimated at about—Say either "about" or "estimated at." The student body is *estimated at* 300. There are *about* 300 students in our school.

He is a man who/She is a woman who—Too many words. All you need to say is "He is . . ." or "She is . . ."

Pair of twins—Avoid this, unless you are referring to two different sets of twins.

The reason is because—Say "the reason is . . ." or "because . . ." *The reason* I want to finish this book is that I need to write a book report. I want to finish this book *because* I have to write a book report.

Too premature, too perfect, really pregnant, very unique—These things either are or aren't. You can't have varying degrees of them. You are either *premature* or you're not. You are either *perfect* or you're not. Well, you get the idea.

The year of 1995—Just say 1995.

True fact—A fact is true. All you need to say is *"fact."*

Cool Books for Cool Readers

Here's a list of books you may actually enjoy. Reading is a surefire way to improve your grammar. But reading stories, novels, and poetry will help you do much more than improve your grammar. You can read for entertainment and for escape. You can also find out about the lives of young people like yourself who have grown up in places, cultures, or time periods different from your own. It's just like going on a trip, except that you don't have to worry about the driving.

The following list includes books recommended by teachers, librarians, and—most important—other young people. Check out the books in your library and take home the ones that seem interesting to you. If you like a book you can ask your parents, friends, teacher, or librarian to recommend others like it. But if you're not hooked after you've read a few chapters of a book, don't worry about it. Try something else. Nobody's grading you!

Adams, Douglas. *The Hitchhiker's Guide to the Galaxy.* (Science Fiction, Humor)
The first book in a series that includes *The Restaurant at the End of the Universe; Life, the Universe & Everything; So Long and Thanks For All the Fish,* and *Mostly Harmless.*

Alcott, Louisa May. *Little Women.* (Classic)

Block, Francesca Lia. *Weetzie Bat.* (Contemporary Fiction)
The first book in a series, which has also been published in the volume *Dangerous Angels: The Weetzie Bat Books.*

Blume, Judy. *Tiger Eyes.* (Contemporary Fiction)
Blume has written many other popular books for young people, including *Blubber* and *Just as Long as We're Together.*

Burnett, Frances Hodgson. *The Secret Garden.* (Classic)

Carroll, Lewis. *Alice's Adventures in Wonderland.* (Classic)
Alice's adventures continue in *Through the Looking Glass.*

Creech, Sharon. *Walk Two Moons.* (Contemporary Fiction)
Creech has written other novels for young people including *Chasing Redbird* and *The Wanderer.*

Cooper, Susan. *The Dark is Rising.* (Fantasy)
The first book in a series that includes *Greenwitch, The Grey King,* and *Silver on the Tree. Over Sea, Under Stone* is the prequel to this series.

Cormier, Robert. *The Chocolate War.* (Contemporary Fiction)

Dorris, Michael. *The Window.* (Contemporary Fiction)
Dorris also wrote about the main character of this novel, Rayona, in his debut novel, *A Yellow Raft in Blue Water.*

Hinton, S. E. *The Outsiders* (Contemporary Fiction)
S. E. Hinton wrote this novel when she was a high school junior.

Fitzgerald, John D. *The Great Brain.* (Historical Fiction)
The first book in a series that includes *More Adventures of the Great Brain, Me and My Little Brain, The Great Brain at the Academy, The Great Brain Reforms, The Return of the Great Brain, The Great Brain Does it Again,* and *The Great Brain Is Back.*

George, Jean Craighead. *Julie of the Wolves.* (Contemporary Fiction)
George has written two other books about Julie, *Julie* and *Julie's Wolf Pack,* as well as *My Side of the Mountain.*

Hughes, Langston. *The Dream Keeper and Other Poems.* (Poetry)

Konigsburg, E. L. *From the Mixed-Up Files of Mrs. Basil E. Frankweiler.* (Contemporary Fiction)

Lee, Gus. *China Boy.* (Contemporary Fiction)
Also read the sequel, *Honor and Duty.*

LeGuin, Ursula. *A Wizard of Earthsea.* (Fantasy)
The first book in a series that includes *A Wizard of Earthsea, The Tombs of Atuan, The Farthest Shore,* and *Tehanu.*

L'Engle, Madeleine. *A Wrinkle in Time.* (Science Fiction, Contemporary Fiction)
L'Engle's series about the Murry family continues in *A Swiftly Tilting Planet, A Wind in the Door, An Acceptable Time,* and *Many Waters.* Also try *A Ring of Endless Light,* a favorite in her series about Vicky Austin and her family.

Lewis, C. S. *The Lion, the Witch, and the Wardrobe.* (Classic, Fantasy)
The first book in the *Chronicles of Narnia.*

Montgomery, Lucy Maude. *Anne of Green Gables.* (Classic)
Anne Shirley's story continues in *Anne of Avonlea* and *Anne of the Island. Rainbow Valley* and *Rilla of Ingleside* are about her children. Also try Montgomery's series about Emily Starr: *Emily of New Moon, Emily Climbs,* and *Emily's Quest.*

Myers, Walter Dean. *Hoops.* (Contemporary Fiction)
Myers has written dozens of books, including *Fallen Angels* and *Monster.*

Nye, Naomi Shihab. *Habibi.* (Contemporary Fiction)

Paterson, Katherine. *Bridge to Terabithia.* (Contemporary Fiction)
Other popular books by Paterson include *The Great Gilly Hopkins, The Master Puppeteer,* and *Jacob Have I Loved.*

Paulsen, Gary. *Nightjohn*. (Historical Fiction)
Paulsen has also written a sequel, *Sarny*, as well as many
adventure books, including *Hatchet*, the first in a series.

Rawls, Wilson. *Where the Red Fern Grows*. (Classic)

Rowling, J. K. *Harry Potter and the Sorcerer's Stone*. (Fantasy)
The first book in a wildly popular series that includes *Harry
Potter and the Chamber of Secrets*, *Harry Potter and the Prisoner of
Azkaban*, and *Harry Potter and the Goblet of Fire*.

Salinger, J. D. *The Catcher in the Rye*. (Classic)

de Saint-Exupery, Antoine. *The Little Prince*. (Classic, Fantasy)

Soto, Gary. *Baseball in April and Other Stories*. (Contemporary
Fiction)
Also try Soto's novel *Crazy Weekend*, and *Neighborhood Odes*, a
collection of his poetry.

Staples, Suzanne Fisher. *Shabanu: Daughter of the Wind*.
(Contemporary Fiction)
Shabanu's story continues in *Haveli*.

Taylor, Mildred D. *Roll of Thunder, Hear My Cry*. (Historical
Fiction)

Tolkien, J. R. R. *The Hobbit*. (Fantasy)
The prequel to the *Lord of the Rings* series, which includes *The
Fellowship of the Ring*, *The Two Towers*, and *The Return of the King*.

Voigt, Cynthia. *Homecoming*. (Contemporary Fiction)
The first book about Dicey Tillerman's family and friends;
others include *Dicey's Song*, *A Solitary Blue*, and *Seventeen
Against the Dealer*.

Wojciechowska, Maia. *Shadow of a Bull*. (Fiction)

Yep, Laurence. *Dragonwings*. (Historical Fiction)
Also try Yep's other novels about Chinese-American life, *Child
of the Owl* and *Dragon's Gate*.

Zindel, Paul. *The Pigman*. (Contemporary Fiction)

Glossary

active voice: when the subject performs the action described by the verb (as compared to the passive voice, when the action described by the verb happens to the subject) (*Mary drove to the store.*)

adjective: a word that describes a noun or a pronoun (*beautiful, smart, nice, happy*)

adverb: a word that describes a verb, an adjective, or another adverb. Adverbs often, but do not always, end in *-ly* (*quickly, very, nicely*)

agreement: a term used either to indicate that the subject must agree with the verb (*he smiles* instead of *he smile*) or that the pronoun must agree with the noun it replaces (*The people want their hamburgers* instead of *The people want his hamburger.*)

appositive: a phrase (usually a noun), set off by commas, that explains something (John, *my best friend,* is getting me tickets to the concert.)

apostrophe: a punctuation mark that shows ownership (*Mark's bicycle*) or a contraction (*don't, won't*) to show that the letters have been left out

article: a special group of adjectives that refer to people, places, ideas, or things. *The, a,* and *an* are articles.

case: form that shows the function of a pronoun. The subjective (or nominative) case pronoun is used in the *subject* of a sentence. The objective case is used in the *object* of a sentence

clause: a group of words with a subject and a verb. Independent clauses may stand alone; dependent clauses may not

collective noun: a group noun that is usually treated as singular in number (*audience, jury, government*)

colon: punctuation mark used to introduce a list or an example and to separate the hours and minutes in the time of day (*We need two things: courage and patience.*)

comma: punctuation mark used for a pause, or to set off part of a sentence for clarity

conjunction: joining word that may act alone or in pairs. *And, but,* and *or* are conjunctions that act alone. *Neither . . . nor, either . . . or,* and *not only . . . but* are conjunctions that work in pairs

dash: a punctuation mark that may be used like a comma or parentheses (*You know—don't you—that I really like to skate.*)

demonstrative pronoun: a pronoun used to point out specific people, places, things, or ideas (*that, these, those, this*)

dependent clause: a group of words with a subject and a verb that would not make sense standing alone as a sentence (*When the boy cried,* his mother came running.)

diction: correct word choice

direct object: the noun that receives the action of the verb in the sentence. (I want to eat *hamburgers.*)

future tense: verb tense used to indicate an action that will happen. Uses the words *will* or *shall*

future perfect tense: verb tense used to show an action that will be finished before a specific time in the future (Before next Wednesday, I *will have* lost five pounds.)

gender: applies to nouns and pronouns that refer to people. It can either be male, female, or neutral (applying to both men and women)

gerund: *-ing* form of a verb, which acts as a noun (*Skating* is great.)

helping verb: words used with the main verb to form tenses (We *will* go to the park. I *have been* trying not to eat ice cream.)

idiom: a phrase that doesn't make sense literally or follow any specific grammar rule. Idioms include funny expressions (*Let a smile be your umbrella.*) and preposition use (*A foot is different from a meter.*)

indefinite pronoun: a pronoun that doesn't stand for a particular noun. *Each, either, any, few, none, some* are indefinite pronouns

independent clause: the main clause of the sentence. It can stand alone, without the dependent clauses (when the boy cried, *his mother came running.*)

indirect object: receiver of the direct object (Give *me* your skates.) that can be turned into a prepositional phrase. (Give your skates to me.)

infinitive: the "to" form of the verb (*to be, to go, to eat*) that is used as a noun, adjective, or adverb

interjection: a word used for emphasis (*Cool! Yikes! Wow! Hey!*)

interrogative pronoun: a pronoun used to ask a question (*Who? What? Which?*)

misplaced modifier: a phrase or word that is not next to the thing it is modifying. It usually makes a sentence unclear

modify: to describe. Adjectives and adverbs are modifiers

nominative case: also called subjective case. The pronoun used if it is the subject of a verb

noun: a person, place, thing, or idea (*bookworm, Denver, house, truth*)

number: term describing whether something is singular or plural.

object: the object of a verb is the thing acted upon by the subject. (I ate *ice cream.*) The object of a preposition is the noun that is being placed by the preposition (We went to *the house.*)

objective case: the form of pronoun that is used as the object of a verb

parallel construction: the rule that when you construct a list, all the things in the list should be in the same form

participle: a verb form that acts as an adjective (Katie couldn't deal with the *annoying* sounds.)

past tense: the verb tense that indicates that something has already happened.

past perfect: the verb tense describing past before the past (Before I went to the dance, I *had gone* to the store.)

period: punctuation mark used at the end of a statement or in abbreviations

person: the term used to categorize personal pronouns. *First person* refers to the speaker: I, we. *Second person* refers to the person being spoken to: you. *Third person* refers to the person being spoken about: he, she, they

phrase: a group of words that work together as one part of speech in a sentence. The main types of phrases are prepositional, infinitive, participial, and gerund

plural: more than one, as opposed to singular. Nouns, pronouns, and verbs may be plural or singular

possessive pronoun: pronoun that shows ownership (*my, his, hers, its, theirs*)

predicate: the part of the sentence that includes the verb and all words related to it

preposition: a word used to place a noun in time or space (*at, toward, around, before, into, after*)

present tense: verb tense used to show that something is happening right now or to state a fact

present perfect: verb tense used to show an action that began in the past, but continues into the present, or was finished at some indefinite, earlier time (I *have lost* fifteen pounds.)

principal parts: the basic forms of the verb that are used for the different tenses. The principal parts include the present, past, and past participle

pronoun: a word base that stands in for a noun (*he, she, it, they*)

question mark: punctuation mark used at the end of a question. (*How are you?*)

quotation mark: punctuation marks used to set off a quote or the title of certain works (*"How are you?" asked Jennifer.*)

redundancy: saying the same thing twice; using unnecessary words

reflexive pronoun: pronoun that refers to the subject. (*He ate it himself.*) It can also be used for emphasis (*I, myself, am outraged.*)

semicolon: punctuation mark used to separate independent clauses in a compound sentence (*I came; I saw; I conquered.*)

singular: refers to nouns and pronouns when there is only one, as opposed to two or more. Singular is also used to refer to the verb that goes with a singular noun or pronoun

subject: the noun or pronoun that performs the action in the sentence. Sometimes it includes descriptive words that come before the noun or pronoun

tense: the form of a verb that tells when an action happened. The six main tenses are present, present perfect, past, past perfect, future, and future perfect

verb: a word that expresses an action or a state of being. You must have a verb to have a sentence (*run, jump, seem, think*)

verbal: a phrase that contains a verb and any modifiers that doesn't act like a verb. The three main types of verbals are gerunds, infinitives, and participles

Answers

✍ **QUIZ #1** ✍
What's this Ticket?

Underline the common nouns and circle the proper nouns in the following passage.

It was a hot <u>day</u> around the old <u>clubhouse</u>. (Sondra) (Barnaby) (Babette) (Taylor) (Bridget) and (Jennifer) had been hanging around watching <u>television</u> most of that <u>week</u>—it seemed too hot to do anything else.

"<u>Man</u>, what I wouldn't do to spend a <u>week</u> on (Gilligan's Island)," said (Barnaby). "First of all, I wouldn't mind meeting the (Professor) and secondly, it sure would be nice and cool there."

"Forget (Gilligan's Island)," answered (Jennifer). "Give me (Friends) any <u>day</u>. I'd love to hang with (Rachel) meet (Joey) bum around with that whole <u>gang</u>. Their <u>lives</u> seem like so much fun."

"You <u>guys</u> are weird." said (Taylor) dreamily. "Give me a nice, happy <u>family</u> like the one on the (Brady Bunch) Now there are some fun <u>people</u> I'd like to spend a <u>week</u> with."

"What's this silver ticket on the floor?" asked Bridget. "I've never seen anything like it before."

A Ticket to Adventure

Underline the pronouns in the following passage.

"It says, 'This is your ticket to adventure. If you hold onto it tightly, you will be transported to the television show of your dreams. To escape from your adventure, say the words *anna banana*,'" said Jennifer.

"That's strange. What do you suppose it means?" wondered Babette.

"I suppose that it means exactly what it says. Where would we like to go?" answered Barnaby, being logical as usual.

"I would like to go to Central Perk to hang out with the cast of *Friends*," Jennifer said. "They would all love me!"

"I don't know about that," said Taylor.

But it was too late. The clubhouse began to rattle. They all held onto the nearest pieces of furniture. Before they could say "Ross and Rachel," they were off.

✍ QUIZ #3 ✍

Friends, Here We Come!

Underline the verbs in the following passage.

Jennifer <u>opened</u> the door slowly. The coffee shop <u>was filled</u> with customers. Soon, the kids <u>heard</u> a familiar voice.

"What <u>is</u> this ugly house <u>doing</u> in Central Perk?" Monica <u>asked</u> harshly.

"Uh, we <u>are</u> not exactly sure ourselves," <u>answered</u> Jennifer. "<u>Is</u> this really Central Perk?"

"You <u>bet</u>, Sweetie," <u>answered</u> Rachel. "And if you <u>don't get</u> this broken-down old clubhouse out of our coffee shop, we <u>will force</u> you out."

"Rachel, what <u>is</u> the problem?" Joey <u>entered</u> the scene.

"No problem, Joey. There <u>is</u> just a bunch of rude, noisy kids <u>trespassing</u> in our cool hangout. I <u>am</u> sure they <u>will find</u> their way out of here before you <u>can wink</u> an eye." Rachel <u>turned</u> on her heel, <u>stomped</u> up to the counter, and <u>ordered</u> a latté.

"Hmm, what <u>do</u> you <u>think</u> of Rachel now?" <u>asked</u> Sondra.

"Ugh," <u>answered</u> Jennifer. "*Anna banana.*"

Just Sit Right Back
and You'll Hear a Tale . . .

Underline the adjectives in the following passage.

The clubhouse may have been <u>shabby</u>, but it was <u>sturdy</u> enough to get them back home in a wink.

"Wow," said Jennifer, "this <u>silver</u> ticket really works! We should think hard about the next <u>exciting</u> place we'd like to go."

"We could go somewhere <u>cool</u>," offered Barnaby.

"Somewhere <u>fun</u>," said Babette.

"Somewhere <u>exotic</u>," said Taylor.

"Hmm, Central Perk wasn't <u>exotic</u> enough for you?" asked a <u>nervous</u> Bridget. She snapped her <u>cherry</u> gum and blew an <u>enormous</u> bubble.

"No, let's try someplace <u>new</u> and <u>different</u>," answered Babette.

"Someplace where there are <u>cool ocean</u> breezes, perhaps?" asked Barnaby.

"Yeah, <u>cool, fresh</u> breezes. That sounds pretty <u>nice</u>." Taylor looked off into the <u>steamy</u> street.

"Maybe *Gilligan's Island*?" Barnaby grabbed the <u>silver</u> ticket and rubbed it.

The Professor and Barnaby

Underline the adverbs in the following passage.

"Gilligan!" yelled Mary Ann. She ran <u>breathlessly</u> up the beach and into the woods.

The kids were perched <u>clumsily</u> in the nearest coconut tree.

"What's the matter, Mary Ann? You seem <u>very</u> upset." Gilligan ran <u>quickly</u> toward her.

"No, it's just that I heard something—a <u>very</u> funny kind of crash. I'm a <u>little</u> scared, Gilligan. Let's go get the Professor."

"The Professor!" whispered Barnaby <u>excitedly</u>. "I have <u>always</u> wanted to meet him. He's one of the great minds in television history."

"Sure, if he's <u>so</u> <u>very</u> smart, how come he <u>never</u> got them off this stupid island?" Bridget snapped her gum <u>furiously</u>.

"Sssh, Bridget, here he comes!" Barnaby pointed at the figure moving <u>slowly</u> through the clump of trees.

"Professor, we're <u>really</u> stuck. Here! Up in this tree!" called Barnaby.

"My, my, how did you kids get stuck up in a coconut tree?" pondered the Professor. "And who are you, anyway? How can we be sure that you aren't a bunch of spies, sent here by some of our enemies?"

"Spies? Professor, I am your <u>very</u> biggest fan," cried Barnaby."

"Oh, <u>really</u>?" asked the Professor. "And how is it that you know my name?"

✍ QUIZ #6 ✍

Court Martial on Gilligan's Island

Circle the prepositions in the following passage.

Once (in) the hut, the kids began to panic. "How did we get ourselves (into) this?" asked Taylor.

"Don't worry—I'll get us out (of) this trouble," Barnaby said with confidence. "I can reason (with) the Professor."

"Okay, kids, we don't know who you are, but we suspect that you are a bunch (of) spies. How else would that you all know our names?" said the Skipper, pacing (around) the room as he spoke.

"I can prove we're not spies!" cried Babette. "I don't know anything about this stupid show! I only watch *Beverly Hills 90210*."

"A likely story!" answered Ginger. "I've been (to) Beverly Hills, of course, and I'm sure it would be very boring to just sit and watch it all day long. Only a spy would do that! They're trying to learn all (of) our customs."

"Let's feed them (to) the crocodiles!" yelled Mary Ann.

"No, let's send them out (on) a raft!" countered the Professor.

"Forget it!" Barnaby rolled his eyes. "*Anna banana.*"

✍ **QUIZ #7** ✍
Wilma!

Underline the conjunctions in the following passage.

"Ugh," Barnaby said, rolling his eyes as they landed back at home. "<u>Neither</u> *Friends* <u>nor</u> *Gilligan's Island* was at all what I'd imagined."

"Maybe we'd better forget all about this ticket <u>and</u> traveling for today," Bridget said as she snapped her gum.

"<u>Not only</u> are you guys boring, <u>but</u> you also lack imagination," Sondra said. "Let's go someplace, I don't know, unreal. How about Bedrock?"

"Where?" asked Taylor. He had never heard of *Gilligan's Island* <u>or</u> Bedrock. This day was beginning to tire him out.

"You know—Fred, Wilma, Betty, <u>and</u> Barney. Bedrock!"

"Barney? You mean that large, purple dinosaur? I don't think so!" Babette wrinkled her nose <u>and</u> threw her hands up in disgust.

"I'm not talking about the purple dinosaur, Babette. I'm talking about Barney from the cartoon *The Flintstones*. C'mon, <u>either</u> you give me that ticket <u>or</u> I'll never speak to you again."

"Here—do what you want—I give up," Babette said, tossing the ticket at Sondra's feet.

I always wanted to meet Wilma <u>and</u> Betty," Sondra said as she rubbed the ticket.

The walls of the clubhouse began to shimmer. The kids felt weird <u>and</u> wobbly. They were turning into cartoon characters!

✍ QUIZ #8 ✍
We Forgot About the Dinosaurs
Ha! Find the interjections! Underline them!

"<u>Wow</u>! Barney," called Fred, "check this out."

"What is it, Fred?" Barney leaned over the stone fence between their houses. "<u>Yikes</u>! What's that?"

"I'm not sure Barn—it looks like some kind of strange wooden house. Who ever heard of a wooden house?"

The kids nervously peered out the window.

"<u>Cool</u>! We're cartoons. Look, Sondra, there's Fred and Barney. They're pointing at us. Wave."

"<u>Hey</u>, you kids. What are you doing in our tree? Wilma! Call the Rock Police!"

"<u>Oh</u>!" Wilma said as she walked out into the yard. "What's going on here, Fred?"

Dino came bounding into the yard. "Yip, yip!" He jumped up at the base of the tree, clawing furiously at the bottom of the clubhouse.

"They don't seem very friendly, either," Sondra said as she shook her head.

"Oh, well, *anna banana.*"

Chapter 1 Review

There are *eight* parts of speech. Can you name them? Give a quick definition and an example of each one.

1. **noun:** names a person, place, thing, or idea
   book, story, love, justice, truth, cat, dog, fish

2. **pronoun:** takes the place of a noun
   he, she, it, they, their, its, mine, myself

3. **verb:** describes action or state of being
   run, dance, seem, appear, think, is, were

4. **adjective:** describes a noun or pronoun
   ugly, pretty, nice, small, big

5. **adverb:** describes a verb, adjective, or another adverb
   quickly, nicely, fast, very, so

6. **preposition:** relates a noun or pronoun to another word in a sentence; usually refers to time and space
   after, before, in, to, out, from, over

7. **conjunction:** joins parts of a sentence

   and, or, but

8. **interjection:** word used for emphasis

   hah!, yikes!, cool!

Use _N_ for noun, _P_ for pronoun, _V_ for verb, _ADJ_ for adjective, _ADV_ for adverb, _PR_ for preposition, _C_ for conjunction, and _I_ for interjection.

1. Rose and Lionel always went to the store
   N   C   N   ADV   V   PR   N

   on Saturday.
   PR   N

2. They wanted to buy some comic books
   P   V   V   V   ADJ ADJ   N

   with their money.
   PR   P   N

3. "Yikes!" cried Lionel. "*X-Men* is on sale."
   I   V   N   N   V PR N

4. I love *X-Men,* but *Spawn* is definitely a
   P V   N   C   N   V   ADV

   great comic.
   ADJ   N

5. *Spawn* and *X-Men* are both excellent.
   N   C   N   V ADJ   ADJ

⚐ QUIZ #9 ⚐
Subjects

Underline the subject in each of the following sentences.

1. <u>Amanda</u> stormed into the room.
2. (<u>You</u>) "Get away from my boyfriend!" (implied subject)
3. "<u>He</u> is not your boyfriend!"
4. <u>Amanda</u> picked up a teddy bear and threw it at Jennifer.
5. Without a moment's hesitation, <u>Jennifer</u> ran out of the room.

⚐ QUIZ #10 ⚐
Springfield, Here We Come!

In the following passage, underline each verb and circle the complete subject that goes with it.

Thump. (The clubhouse) <u>landed</u> back in Babette's yard.

"(I) <u>am</u> glad we got to be (cartoons)," Sondra <u>said</u>. "(I) sure <u>did like</u> that feeling."

"Well, (we) <u>have had</u> a very exciting day so far, but (we) <u>have been</u> somewhat unlucky in our choices," (Barnaby) <u>said</u>.

"Listen, guys, (you) just <u>don't know</u> how to pick fun places," (Bridget) <u>said</u>. (She) <u>blew</u> a huge bubble and <u>was lifted</u> off the ground a few inches. "Why (don't we)(visit the Simpsons in Springfield?(We)(will have) fun there.(Bart)(is a riot.(Maggie)(is) so cute. (You)(Give) me that ticket."

"Great!(We)(can be) cartoon characters again," (Sondra)(said).

(Bridget)(rubbed) the ticket while humming the theme song to *The Simpsons*.(The clubhouse) <u>began to shake</u> once more.

✍ QUIZ #11 ✍
Who's Trespassing in Springfield?

Underline the complete subject and put parentheses around the complete predicate in each of the following sentences.

<u>The water</u> (began to bubble up around their feet.) <u>The clubhouse</u> (was barely floating.)

"<u>We</u>('ve landed in a swimming pool!") <u>Bridget</u> (wailed.) ("What are) <u>we</u> (going to do?")

"Well, <u>we</u> (should probably get out this clubhouse pronto,") <u>Barnaby</u> (suggested.)

<u>Jennifer</u> (peered out the window.) "<u>I</u> (don't think that is a very good idea, Barnaby.")

("Why would) <u>you</u> (say that, Jennifer?) <u>We</u> (happen to be sinking.")

"Yeah, well <u>I</u> (think) (I would rather drown.") <u>Jennifer</u> (pointed out the window.)

"It('s Chief Wiggum and the Springfield Police!") Bridget (yelled.)

("What are) you kids (doing in the Simpsons' swimming pool?") Chief Wiggum (bellowed on a bullhorn.) "All right, you kids (come out with your hands up.")

("*Anna banana!*") they all (yelled at once.)

✍ QUIZ #12 ✍
Complete Sentences

Mark the complete sentences with an "S." Mark the fragments with an "F."

1. Granny marched into the room. S
2. After looking at the time, left to find Jed. F
3. Sniffling and crying in the corner. F
4. Elly Mae was a mess. S
5. Jethro couldn't help but notice what a mess Elly Mae was. S

✍ QUIZ #13 ✍
Prepositional Phrases

Find the prepositional phrase or phrases in each sentence. Put parentheses around them.

1. (At the house), Sydney put some ice (on her nose).
2. Jake, who was (in the kitchen), asked her if she wanted some soda.

3. Amanda, Sydney, and Jake were pretty shaken up (after the incident).

4. As always, Amanda felt triumphant (in her apartment).

5. Back (at the pool) Billy was getting ready (for a swim).

✍ QUIZ #14 ✍
Phrases and Clauses

Each of the following sentences contains one or two clauses. Underline the dependent clauses and put parentheses around the independent clauses.

1. After the party, (Alison called Jane.)

2. <u>Unless you were there</u>, (you wouldn't believe it!)

3. (Jane called her sister) <u>before she found out</u>.

4. (Sydney told Jake) about the incident.

5. <u>When he returned</u>, (Billy spoke to Amanda.)

✍ QUIZ #15 ✍
Compound Sentences

Rewrite each of these simple sentences as one compound sentence.

1. Amanda came home. She found Billy on her couch.

Amanda came home and found Billy on her couch.

2. Billy told her to cool out. He would leave.

   Billy told her to cool out or he would leave.

3. I want to cool out! She won't let me!

   I want to cool out but she won't let me!

4. He ate pizza. It was his favorite food.

   He ate pizza because it was his favorite food.

5. He ate it every day. It was fattening.

   He ate it every day even though it was fattening.

6. He ate the pizza. She ate brownies.

   He ate the pizza and she ate brownies.

Now turn the following complicated, confusing sentences into one or two simple sentences.

7. JuJu fruits, which are red, are the most nutritious.

   Red JuJu fruits are the most nutritious.

8. If you are going to San Francisco, which can be very foggy, make sure you bring your flashlight.

   If you are going to foggy San Francisco, make sure you bring your flashlight.

9. Eating hot dogs can be great, but Maria ate fifteen every day for lunch and soon began to feel sick about the whole thing.

Eating hot dogs can be great. However, Maria ate fifteen every day for lunch and soon began to feel sick about the whole thing.

✍ QUIZ #16 ✍
Putting It All Together

In the following sentences, circle the verbs and underline the subjects. Also, mark "S" if it is a simple sentence, "C" if it is a compound sentence, and "X" if it is a complex sentence.

1. Jennifer asked Sondra what it was that she wanted. X

2. I need help! S

3. Barnaby and Sondra offered to buy Bridget some fresh bubble gum. S

4. Do you think this ticket is so bad, even though we've had some misadventures? C

5. After she thought about it, Bridget was convinced that her friends were right.

6. We've had some problems, but I still think this could be fun. C

7. (We) Let's go! S

8. We will be together. S

9. We've had some bad luck, but we will try again. C

✐ QUIZ #17 ✐
Singular and Plural Nouns

Change the singular nouns in parentheses to plural nouns.

1. Sondra asked Jennifer to eat fifteen <u>bananas</u>.
2. Taylor told me that his twelve <u>monkeys</u> escaped from their <u>cages</u> and wanted to wash their <u>feet</u> in the bath.
3. My favorite <u>movies</u> are <u>comedies</u>.
4. If you are going to put <u>foxes</u> in <u>boxes</u>, you'd better not bring them to <u>churches</u> or feed them <u>lunches</u>.
5. The shoemaker's <u>elves</u> put the <u>shoes</u> on the <u>shelves</u> all by themselves.
6. One of the great <u>joys</u> of eating <u>burgers</u> is that you don't need <u>knives</u>.
7. "Do you know where the <u>ladies</u> who sold me these <u>shoes</u> are?" asked Babette.
8. "I believe they are hiding in the <u>bushes</u> or behind that group of <u>men</u>," Taylor replied.
9. If you clear the <u>dishes</u> from the table, make sure you wrap the <u>leftovers</u> and put the <u>bowls</u> in the refrigerator.
10. If you take out the <u>paints</u>, wash the <u>paintbrushes</u> before you use them.

✍ QUIZ #18 ✍
Possessives
Fill in the missing parts of the following chart.

Singular	Singular Possessive	Plural	Plural Possessive
berry	berry's	berries	berries'
cat	cat's	cats	cats'
desk	desk's	desks	desks'
dog	dog's	dogs	dogs'
family	family's	families	families'
glove	glove's	gloves	gloves'
house	house's	houses	houses'
Jones	Jones's	Joneses	Joneses'
peach	peach's	peaches	peaches'
thief	thief's	thieves	thieves'

✍ QUIZ #19 ✍
Finding Direct and Indirect Objects
In each of the following sentences, circle the direct object and underline the indirect object (if one exists).

1. Dylan told <u>Brenda</u> the bad (news.)
2. Brenda sold <u>Tiffani</u> (rights) to the story.
3. The police asked <u>Dylan</u> several (questions.)
4. We wanted (bananas) and peeled (grapes) for the party.
5. Brandon ate ninety-eight (bananas) before winning the contest.

✍ QUIZ #20 ✍
Identifying Predicate Nouns

Underline the predicate nouns in the following sentences.

1. Bart is an intrepid <u>explorer</u>.
2. Always afraid of his shadow, Mr. Burns is a <u>coward</u>.
3. That <u>kid</u> with the glasses is Milhouse.
4. Maggie is the youngest <u>child</u>.
5. Homer seems like a new <u>man</u>.

✍ QUIZ #21 ✍
Babette in the Big City

Underline the correct pronoun in each of the following sentences.

After returning from Springfield, Barnaby looked at Babette. (<u>He</u>, Him) wanted to know what (<u>she</u>, her) thought of that trip.

"Darling, that place was a dump, believe (I, <u>me</u>). New York City is a place where there's some real action. We can meet the cast of *Seinfeld:* Jerry, Elaine, Kramer, and George. That George is a cutie pie. Let (<u>us</u>, we) go there," Babette cried.

"Do you think (us, <u>we</u>) really should try again?" (<u>they</u>, them) all wondered aloud.

"(Us, <u>We</u>) will never know unless (us, <u>we</u>) try again!" Babette told (they, <u>them</u>).

"Between you and (I, <u>me</u>)," Jennifer whispered to Bridget, "(<u>I</u>, me) don't care if (<u>I</u>, me) ever see New York City."

"Give (I, <u>me</u>) the ticket, darling," Babette ordered. "Oh, George, (<u>I</u>, me) can't wait to meet you."

The clubhouse rumbled. Thwump! (<u>They</u>, Them) landed in Jerry's apartment.

"Who's there?" (<u>they</u>, them) heard a voice call from the kitchen.

✑ QUIZ #22 ✑
Relative Pronoun Practice

Underline the correct relative pronoun in each of the following sentences.

1. Sideshow Bob, (<u>who</u>, whom) is Krusty's faithful sidekick, was after Bart.

2. *The Krusty the Clown Show*, (<u>which</u>, that) is Lisa's favorite, is on at 4 P.M. each day.

3. The *Itchy and Scratchy* episode (which, <u>that</u>) Bart and Lisa like the best is quite gory.

4. Could these be the children (who, <u>whom</u>) I brought into the world?

5. Maggie's favorite pacifier is the one (<u>that</u>, which) makes the most noise.

✍ QUIZ #23 ✍
Pronoun Agreement

Cross out the incorrect pronoun in each sentence and replace it with a better one.

1. Either Ginger or Mary Ann was sure to have brought <u>her</u> new bathing suit.

2. Anybody who has seen *Gilligan's Island* is certain to know that <u>he or she</u> has seen a classic.

3. "If anyone finds a way off this island, would <u>she or he</u> please let us know?" cried Mr. Howell.

4. "Oh, Thurston," called Mrs. Howell, "neither Gilligan nor you is able to figure out what <u>he</u> really wants."

5. "All of <u>us</u> are happy as clams to be here. We want to stay on this island forever!" cried Mary Ann.

✍ QUIZ #24 ✍
Subject-Verb Agreement

Match the correct verb with the subject in the following sentences. Underline each correct verb.

1. Alice <u>cooks</u> for the kids every night.

2. Every night, she <u>makes</u> their favorite meal: meatloaf.

3. "<u>Weren't</u> we going to have something different tonight, Alice?" <u>asks</u> Cindy.

4. "Yikes! Meatloaf again!" <u>cry</u> Jan and Marcia. "We need some variety!"

5. "<u>Don't</u> you people have anything better to do than worry about dinner?" <u>wonders</u> Alice.

6. "Oh, no, not meatloaf!" <u>yells</u> Mr. Brady from upstairs.

7. "Oh, I <u>am</u> sick of trying to please all of you finicky Bradys!" Alice says as she <u>stomps</u> out of the house for the last time.

✍ QUIZ #25 ✍

Mr. Brady! Save us from George!

Change all the present tense verbs that don't make sense to the past tense. Rewrite the passage in the space provided after it.

George *came* into Jerry's living room and *saw* the clubhouse. The kids *shook* when they *heard* him yell and scream. "This clubhouse! Why *did* it *land* in Jerry's apartment?"

Babette *looked* out of the window. "What a hunk!" she *cried*. "But he is being so violent. I am scared."

"Get out of here, or I'll call the police."

"Quick, give me the ticket. I have an idea," Taylor *said*. He *rubbed* the ticket and *cried*, "Help us, Mr. Brady!"

Suddenly, Mr. Brady *walked* into the apartment. "Hey!" he *yelled*, "stop hitting that clubhouse!"

George *turned* around. "This is my friend's apartment. I'm watching it for him, so I'll hit whatever I want."

"Excuse me, kids, but who lives here?"

"His friend does," Babette *pointed* sheepishly toward George.

"Sorry, bud. My mistake." Mr. Brady *picked* up a golf club and *waved* it at the clubhouse with George. "Okay, you kids, get out of here or I'll have to call the police."

"*Anna banana*!" Taylor *threw* his hands up in disgust.

✍ QUIZ #26 ✍
Tenses

Fill in the correct verb form in each blank. The verb is in the infinitive form at the end of each sentence.

1. Yesterday, Barnaby *ate* twenty-seven chocolate chip cookies. (to eat)

2. Before he finished the cookies, he *had baked* four dozen. (to bake)

3. Right now, Bridget *chews* her favorite bubble gum. (to chew)

4. Tomorrow, Barnaby and Bridget *will go* to Jennifer's house. (to go)

5. By next Wednesday, Barnaby *will have baked* another thirty batches of chocolate chip cookies. (to bake)

6. Mr. James said that he *will cut* the budget for WNYX next month. (to cut)

7. Dave and Lisa's productivity *dropped* after they had stopped dating. (to drop)

8. Johnny Johnson was sent to jail after he *had threatened* to take over Jimmy's empire. (to threaten)

9. After wondering why everyone was giggling at him all day, Beth *told* Matthew that someone had taped the word "Spaz" to the back of his sweater. (to tell)

10. Joe *builds* crazy gadgets out of duct tape and clay in his spare time. (to build)

✍ QUIZ #27 ✎
Correct Verb Forms

Underline the correct form of the verb in each sentence.

1. Max (<u>wept</u>, weeped) when he heard the bad news.

2. "My brother has (grew, <u>grown</u>)," he said.

3. "I have (laid, <u>lain</u>) on my bed too long!" she exclaimed.

4. "If I had (tore, <u>torn</u>) that piece of paper, no one would have found out."

5. "I (brang, <u>brought</u>) this on myself," thought Rosa.

6. Mr. McMahon (<u>swore</u>, sworn) that his daughter Stephanie would never marry a wrestler.

7. Kurt Angle (hanged, <u>hung</u>) his Olympic gold medals on his bedroom wall.

8. Many competitors have (froze, <u>frozen</u>) in fear at the sight of "Stone Cold" Steve Austin.

9. The match began when the timekeeper (<u>rang</u>, rung) the bell.

10. The Rock had been (<u>shaken</u>, shook) after the Undertaker hit him with a chair.

✍ QUIZ #28 ✍
Find the Participles

Put parentheses around the participles in the following sentences.

1. When he discovered his (missing) barbecued ribs, Vince called for Linda.

2. Christian used the peaches (picked) from the tree to bake a pie.

3. Mr. Austin thought that Shane's answer was wrong because it included a (misspelled) word.

4. It is a great convenience to have (running) water.

5. There were so many (screaming) children in the movie.

✍ QUIZ #29 ✍
Spotting Gerunds

Underline the gerunds in each of the following sentences.

1. I always liked <u>playing</u> baseball.
2. We all enjoyed <u>running</u> out onto the field.
3. <u>Batting</u> is the one thing I don't do that well.
4. <u>Fielding</u> is my area of expertise.
5. <u>Winning</u>, however, is something everybody likes.

✍ QUIZ #30 ✍
Infinitives

Underline the infinitive in each of the following sentences.

1. Jethro wanted <u>to see</u> the sights in Beverly Hills.
2. <u>To go</u> to the races was Granny's favorite pastime.
3. Mr. Drysdale wanted <u>to eat</u> with the Clampetts.

4. Elly Mae hoped <u>to win</u> the beauty contest that week.

5. Milhouse always has <u>to run</u> from Jimbo after school.

6. Ralph waits until the teacher is out of the room before he starts <u>to eat</u> paste.

7. "<u>To work</u> at the DMV is no picnic," Patty said to Selma.

✍ QUIZ #31 ✍
Comparative Forms of Adjectives

Underline the correct adjective form in the following sentences.

1. Of all the kids, Barnaby was the <u>smartest</u>.

2. Taylor was <u>quieter</u> than Jennifer.

3. Instead of yummy mashed potatoes or healthy string beans, Bridget likes bubble gum <u>best</u>.

4. Between Sondra and Taylor, Sondra is the <u>odder</u> person.

5. Babette is the <u>most</u> mysterious person you have ever met.

✍ QUIZ #32 ✍
Adjectives and Adverbs

Underline the correct words in each of the following sentences.

1. Amanda felt <u>well</u> on that <u>beautiful</u> day.

2. Jake wanted <u>badly</u> to call her and tell her how <u>sad</u> he felt.

3. Sydney told her sister that she dressed <u>well</u> for such a <u>good</u> day.

4. After coming to a <u>sudden</u> stop, Jake's <u>new</u> car screeched <u>loudly</u>.

5. Stomping <u>forcefully</u> out of the room, Amanda flipped her <u>thick</u> blonde hair out of her <u>cool</u> eyes.

✍ QUIZ #33 ✍
Misplaced Modifiers

Underline the misplaced modifier, and then rewrite each of the following sentences.

1. <u>Approaching his favorite TV star</u>, admiration was oozing out of Barnaby.

   Approaching his favorite TV star, Barnaby was oozing admiration.

2. <u>Hearing the voice of Wilma</u>, a wave of excitement came over Sondra.

   Hearing the voice of Wilma, Sondra felt a wave of excitement.

3. <u>Going to the set of the TV show *Friends*</u>, the ride was bumpy for Babette.

    The ride was bumpy for Babette when she went to the set of the TV show *Friends*.

4. <u>Thinking about Rachel</u>, a pole was walked into by a dreamy Jennifer.

    Thinking about Rachel, a dreamy Jennifer walked into a pole.

✍ QUIZ #34 ✍
Preposition Time

Underline the correct preposition in each of the following sentences.

1. Tom went <u>to</u> Michael's Pet Store yesterday.

2. You know, Tom is really very different <u>from</u> Michael.

3. When Tom bought that fish <u>from</u> Michael, we were all very surprised.

4. <u>Besides</u> Tom, Michael doesn't have many friends.

5. <u>Between</u> Michael and Tom, Tom is more friendly.

6. Tom was upset <u>with</u> Michael for selling him such a boring pet.

✍ QUIZ #35 ✍
Faulty Comparisons

Correct the error in each of the following sentences.

1. "I love Mary Ann's smile so much more than Ginger's <u>smile</u>!" cried Barnaby.

2. "That may be true, but the storyline of *Friends* is far better than <u>the storyline of</u> *Gilligan's Island*," shrieked Jennifer.

3. "The storyline may be better, but Rachel's character is not nearly as nice as Mary Ann's <u>character</u>," answered Babette.

4. "Rachel's dresses are far more stylish than Mary Ann's <u>dresses</u>," offered Taylor.

5. "Perhaps, but I still think that Mary Ann's hair is much prettier than Rachel's <u>hair</u>," whispered Barnaby.

✍ QUIZ #36 ✍
Parallel Construction

Correct the error in each of the following sentences.

1. The castaways had tried many different ways to get off the island: building rafts, signaling with flares, and <u>calling ships with their radio.</u>

2. Fred and Wilma were hosting the annual company picnic. They fried brontosaurus burgers, grilled stegosaurus ribs, and <u>barbecued hot dogs</u> as well.

3. Amanda wanted to be successful, make a lot of money, and <u>build a great empire.</u>

4. Warning: Watching too much television can damage your brain, cause eye strain, and <u>interfere with your ability to read.</u>

5. After eating, jumping rope, and <u>swimming,</u> the gang went back to the clubhouse.

✍ QUIZ #37 ✍
Anna Banana, We're Home!

Punctuate the following passage. Remember that there is some flexibility here, but do your best and try to keep the paragraph clear.

Barnaby, Babette, Sondra, Taylor, and Jennifer were all quite tired but exhilarated nonetheless.

"The Professor was not quite as smart as I'd always hoped, but it was neat to finally see him anyway," Barnaby said.

"Maybe you're right about the Professor," said Jennifer, "but no one could compare to Rachel and her amazing clothes."

"Are you kidding? She was so mean," said Taylor.

"I think we all had some pretty exciting adventures," said Jennifer, "but I, for one, am happy to be back here. All that fighting and drama has worn me out."

"Yes," agreed Taylor. "I don't think I would really want to be in *The Brady Bunch* after all."

"I would definitely not want to be a part of that stupid *Seinfeld* show," said Babette. "I am very glad to be home."

The gang soon realized one thing—being part of a television show would be pretty exhausting after awhile.

"Let's burn that ticket," said Taylor. "It's the only safe, reasonable thing to do."

"I think he is right," said Barnaby. "Logically speaking, of course, we should cut our losses and just hang here despite the great heat."

They made a ceremonial fire and watched the silver ticket crumple and burn.

"There's no place like home!" cried Bridget.

✍ QUIZ #38 ✍
Diction

Underline the correct word or words in each of the following sentences.

1. After returning from her adventures, Bridget was so tired, she was barely <u>intelligible</u>.

2. We need to buy some paper from the <u>stationery</u> store and write all this down.

3. "<u>You're</u> kidding, right?" said Barnaby. "<u>It's</u> <u>too</u> unbelievable."

4. "That stupid ticket sure was <u>irritating</u>. We hardly had <u>any</u> good luck," growled Jennifer.

5. "If we had <u>fewer</u> adventures, we wouldn't have anything fun to talk about," Sondra pointed out.

6. "We should have <u>sneaked</u> past George and gone to find Jerry," Babette pouted.

7. "Well, I am going to <u>lie</u> down now and take a nap. That was exhausting," Barnaby said.

ABOUT THE AUTHOR

Liz Buffa joined The Princeton Review in 1989. She has taught classes in SAT, LSAT, GMAT, and SAT-II special subject tests. She is a graduate of Wellesley College and lives in Locust Valley, N.Y., with her husband and two sons, David and Paul. This is her third book for The Princeton Review.

KIRKWOOD

The Princeton Review

Award-Winning

Smart Junior Guides

for Kids in Grades 6–8

Math Smart JUNIOR
Math You'll ...tand
• Learn decimals from ...

Wor...
Build a Straight "A" Vocabulary

C. L. Brantley

GRAMMAR SMART JR., 2ND EDITION
0-375-76259-0 • $12.00

MATH SMART JR., 2ND EDITION
0-375-76260-4 • $12.00

...)

...ON
...

...TION

...TION

9-27-06

AVA...   ...LD